Strategies for Studying

M. Coles and C. White

COLLINS EDUCATIONAL

Acknowledgements

The publishers are grateful to the following sources for permission to reproduce photographs in this book.

Ian Gibson-Smith, pages 20, 38, 51, 53, 60, 64, 86, 89 and 109
The National Trust, page 63
John Topham Picture Library, pages 19, 25, 26, 39, 66, 92, 93

The publishers have made every effort to trace copyright holders, but if they have inadvertently overlooked any they will be pleased to make the necessary arrangements at the first opportunity.

© M. Coles and C. White 1985

First published 1985 by Collins Educational
8 Grafton Street, London W1X 3LA

ISBN 0 00 322031–1 non-net
ISBN 0 00 197284–7 net

Designed, typeset and illustrated by
DP Press, Sevenoaks, Kent

Printed in Great Britain by
R.J. Acford, Chichester

0 1 2 3 4 5 6 7 8 9 10

British Library Cataloguing in Publication Data
Coles, M.
    Strategies for studying.
    1. Study, Method of
    I. Title   II. White, C.
    371.3′028′12   LB1049

ISBN 0–00–197284–7

Contents

Introduction

The fact that you're now reading this book suggests that you would like to find out how you could improve your study methods.

When you take up study after sixteen you do so voluntarily. You expect to consider subjects in greater depth, and you will be expected to work independently. Many students, however, find difficulty in adapting to advanced study because they have acquired passive study habits.

Up to the age of sixteen you *had* to study and your teachers clearly directed the work. To take just one example, at school you probably experienced a great deal of note-taking (copied and dictated notes) but not very much note-making (arranging ideas for yourself).

This book is based on an extensive survey of approaches to study, and many quotations from students appear in italics.

You have already shown that you would like to become a better student. *Strategies for Studying* will make you aware of your potential, so that you can quickly make progress and enjoy your studies more.

Skim this book to see how you can become an active, independent learner.

1 Start here

Why should I change my study methods? I've already passed some exams. I know what suits me best.

Each **individual** does study in her or his own way. But students over 16 will often have acquired their study habits haphazardly. In this book you will learn about methods which students have found to be particularly effective.

I've had plenty of advice but it doesn't seem to work for me!

Yes, advice has its limitations, but this book offers more – it **demonstrates** how these techniques work. By trying the suggestions in this book you will be able to **compare** them to your present habits and to **select** the methods which suit you best.

Do I have to read the whole book through?

No. Read the first two sections, and then choose which parts are going to meet your needs.

2 Study after sixteen

"If I were starting my sixth form course again I would get myself organized."

"If I were beginning again at college I would think more about preparing myself for the different type of study."

Studying after sixteen is a completely different experience from working in the fifth form, partly because the material is more advanced, but also because you are expected to approach it in quite a new way – as an adult who can organize her or his own learning.

Students who are aware of this are able to prepare for the change and take it in their stride. For example a traveller who knows her destination and arrival time can decide on the means and time of travel to suit herself. If, however, you set off and are not quite sure of where you are going, or when you have to be there, then it is easy to be sidetracked. At first you may enjoy the trip and its detours until you suddenly realise you have very little time left to travel a long way. Panic and last minute rush don't help, and you may find you've missed the boat.

"I would start working hard right from the beginning so that at the end I'd be confident of getting good grades instead of just hoping."

Here are some comments by students on the differences between studying in the fifth year and studying after 16. Note in the margin your reaction to these comments. Which do you strongly agree or disagree with?

"In the fifth year we were spoon-fed, i.e. by dictation."

"It is difficult at first to use your initiative as previously in school you have always been ordered to do homework."

"At the college you don't just have to learn but you have to understand as well."

"It can be more tedious and boring, perhaps because of the less varied course and the longer lessons."

"You are left to study more on your own. You are not chased for work – if it is not done it is your lookout."

"Homework consists of lengthy essays rather than bitty questions to be given in the next day."

> *You are generally treated, often for the first time, as a responsible mature person.*

> *Unless it's what you're really interested in, the work can be mind-bendingly boring.*

> *The work is much more analytical, and you have to think for yourself.*

> *There's more discussion with students giving their opinion, rather than being told everything by the teacher.*

> *Reading around the subject becomes an important part of the course.*

> *There's more work and pressure but also more freedom.*

> *Nobody forces you to do the work.*

> *You are generally treated, often for the first time, as a responsible mature person.*

> *There is the impression that someone may be beginning to think about regarding you as nearly a person.*

3 Are you satisfied with your study habits?

It is important to compare yourself not to some kind of ideal student – they don't exist – but to the best you yourself can achieve. This means that you will be able to set *realistic* targets for yourself.

Read the questions below then underline the appropriate response.

A Attitudes and approaches to study

1 Do you keep an aim in mind when studying?   Yes/No/Sometimes

2 Is the energy you put into your studies adequately rewarded by the results you achieve? Yes/No/Sometimes

3 Do you find it enjoyable to study?   Yes/No/Sometimes

4 Are you satisfied with your study habits?   Yes/No/Partly

B Concentration

1 Do you find it difficult to make a start on your work?   Yes/No/Sometimes

2 Are you easily distracted from your studies?   Yes/No/Sometimes

C Organisation

1 Do you know at what time of the day you work best?   Yes/No

2 Do you set aside regular times for study each week?   Yes/No/Sometimes

3 Do you spread your study periods over the week?   Yes/No/Sometimes

4 Do you tackle the most important and urgent tasks first?   Yes/No/Sometimes

5 Do you take planned breaks?   Yes/No/Sometimes

6 Do you keep up to date with homework assignments?   Yes/No/Sometimes

7 Do you divide your time equally between your different subjects?   Yes/No/Sometimes

8 Have you got somewhere convenient to study?   Yes/No

9 Do you waste time looking for pens and equipment, notes and files?   Yes/No/Sometimes

D Psychology of study

1 Do you reward yourself after finishing a task?   Yes/No/Sometimes

2 Do you know something about the psychology of study?   Yes/No/A little

3 Do you understand how memory works?   Yes/No

E Libraries

1 Do you understand how a library works?   Yes/No/Partly

2 Are you aware of all the services a library can offer you?   Yes/No

3 Can you find information quickly?   Yes/No

F Notes

1 Are your notes easy to understand?   Yes/No

2 Are your notes daunting to revise from?   Yes/No

G Essays

1 Are your essays well planned and coherently argued?   Yes/No/Sometimes

2 Do you tend to repeat yourself in essays?   Yes/No/Sometimes

3 Do you tell the story of something instead of analysing the topic?   Yes/No/Sometimes

4 Are you able to distinguish between main ideas and supporting details or evidence?   Yes/No/Sometimes

H Reading and books

1 Have you done any background reading for your subjects?   Yes/No/A little

2 Do you find it takes you a long time to read a recommended book?   Yes/No

3 Do you read all books in exactly the same way?   Yes/No

4 Do you understand how to use a dictionary and thesaurus properly?   Yes/No/Partly

5 Can you interpret data accurately?   Yes/No

I Revision and exams

1 Do you leave revision till it's too late?   Yes/No/Sometimes

2 Do you panic at exam time?   Yes/No/Sometimes

3 Do you find it difficult to interpret the wording of exam questions?   Yes/No/Sometimes

4 Do you run out of time in exams?   Yes/No/Sometimes

> Analysing your strengths and weaknesses is the first step to improving your study habits.

Each individual will respond differently to this questionnaire. Here are just three responses together with a comment about each.

Sarah

I feel a bit depressed. I don't seem to be doing anything right.

There are no right and wrong ways to study, but if you experiment with the strategies outlined in this book you'll be able to choose those which *you* find most efficient, instead of simply using methods which you have acquired by chance.

Craig

Its certainly made me think, mainly about the importance of organization – I've always taken things as they come up to now. One or two things, like the Essay section, don't apply to me.

Being able to organise your time marks the transition from being a pupil to becoming a student. It is difficult, because as a pupil your teachers organized all your time in school and structured your homework. It's very easy to waste your free time.

Of course not all the sections in this book will apply to you. You don't have to read the book from page 1 to the end; instead decide which sections are relevant and work on them.

Carol

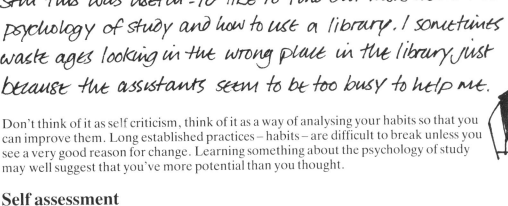

I find it hard to complete this sort of self analysis
– I suppose because it means I have to be self critical.
Still this was useful – I'd like to find out more about the
psychology of study and how to use a library. I sometimes
waste ages looking in the wrong place in the library just
because the assistants seem to be too busy to help me.

Don't think of it as self criticism, think of it as a way of analysing your habits so that you can improve them. Long established practices – habits – are difficult to break unless you see a very good reason for change. Learning something about the psychology of study may well suggest that you've more potential than you thought.

Self assessment

Analyse below your own responses to the questionnaire.

. . . .
. . . .
. . . .
. . . .
. . . .
. . . .
. . . .

4 Organization and planning

1 At college or school

> *You have to learn to study in free time, and not waste the period chatting.*

> *Get your priorities right.*

> Seek out somewhere quiet, perhaps the library, where you can settle to your work without distractions.

2 At home

> *Plan social activities after work.*

> *Don't set yourself goals which are almost impossible to reach.*

> *Never study on a Friday evening. Start afresh on a Saturday morning.*

> *Have one day off completely at the weekend. There is no need to become a recluse.*

> *Try to do your homework early in the evening so that later you have time to relax and rest your brain before going to bed.*

Do you agree with all these comments?

. . . .

. . . .

What conclusions have you reached about the best times for you to study?

. . . .

. . . .

3 Are you making the best use of your time?

People work best at different times: for some the early morning is when they feel freshest, while others find that working late at night suits them.

In either case it is essential to see if you are making the best use of your time. A planner will help you to meet your study targets. First you must look at how you spend your time now. Fill in Study Week Planner I, page 12 as accurately as possible. Leave out lectures and lessons but do put in

    Private study and homework
    Plans and commitments: e.g. sport, clubs, household jobs, a concert, a particular TV
    programme, a disco
    Free time

Now you can see how much time you spend on each.

RECORD SHEET

Study week planner 1: Your current pattern of study

	7-9am	9-11am	11am-1pm	1-3pm	3-5pm	5-7pm	7-9pm	9-11pm
SAT								
SUN								

	7-9am	9am-3pm	3-5pm	5-7pm	7-9pm	9-11pm
MON		Attending				
TUE						
WED						
THU						
FRI						

16	16	16	16	16
17	17	17	17	17
18	18	18	18	18
19	19	19	19	19
20	20	20	20	20
21	21	21	21	21
22	22	22	22	22
23	23	23	23	23
24	24	24	24	24
25	25	25	25	25
26	26	26	26	26
27	27	27	27	27
28	28	28	28	28
29	29	29	29	29
30	30	30	30	30
31		31		31

16	16	16	16	16	16
17	17	17	17	17	17
18	18	18	18	18	18
19	19	19	19	19	19
20	20	20	20	20	20
21	21	21	21	21	21
22	22	22	22	22	22
23	23	23	23	23	23
24	24	24	24	24	24
25	25	25	25	25	25
26	26	26	26	26	26
27	27	27	27	27	27
28	28	28	28	28	28
29	29	29	29	29	29
30	30	30	30	30	
	31		31	31	

Study year planner

SEPTEMBER	OCTOBER	NOVEMBER	DECEMBER	JANUARY	FEBRUARY
1	1	1	1	1	1
2	2	2	2	2	2
3	3	3	3	3	3
4	4	4	4	4	4
5	5	5	5	5	5
6	6	6	6	6	6
7	7	7	7	7	7
8	8	8	8	8	8
9	9	9	9	9	9
10	10	10	10	10	10
11	11	11	11	11	11
12	12	12	12	12	12
13	13	13	13	13	13
14	14	14	14	14	14

Study year planner

MARCH	APRIL	MAY	JUNE	JULY	AUGUST
1	1	1	1	1	1
2	2	2	2	2	2
3	3	3	3	3	3
4	4	4	4	4	4
5	5	5	5	5	5
6	6	6	6	6	6
7	7	7	7	7	7
8	8	8	8	8	8
9	9	9	9	9	9
10	10	10	10	10	10
11	11	11	11	11	11
12	12	12	12	12	12
13	13	13	13	13	13
14	14	14	14	14	14

Complete this table

	Hours, minutes a week
Private study & homework	
Plans and commitments	
Free time	

Are you making the best use of your time?

A study timetable
1 Gives you a target to aim for
2 Spreads your study throughout the week
3 Helps you to establish a routine for study
4 Encourages you to keep up with the work. It is depressing to fall behind, and it is difficult to catch up
5 Saves time in decision making, and lets you get down to things

Check off the points as you plan your next week's study on Study Week Planner 2, page 15. ☑

Note things that you must do	☐
Plan at least 15 hours study/homework over 7 days (18-22 hours at exam time)	☐
Study periods of less than 15 minutes aren't of much use	☐
Most students find it helpful to take a short break about every half hour	☐
Set definite times for starting and finishing your work	☐
Have something to look forward to after a study session – meeting or phoning friends, watching TV or going out, are all suitable rewards.	☐

Making a timetable every week would be a chore, but if you persevere for a few weeks then you will establish the habits of
1 Planning ahead
2 Using your time effectively
and these will become part of your approach to study.

After just a few weeks you will know your best times for study.

4 Homework

' *The work which has to be handed in earliest should be tackled first, even if it is the hardest.* '

' *A pile of work is often daunting when considered as a mass. Break it down into manageable chunks.* '

' *Do the hard things first, while you're still fresh.* '

' *The longer it's left, the harder it is to do.* '

' *If you don't get into the habit of doing regular work at home you'll find it much harder to revise near exam time.* '

' *I find it a great help to make a list of the separate homeworks I need to do then put them in order, and cross them off when I finish them. This way I can see I am getting somewhere.* '

' *Don't let it pile up.* '

Do you disagree with any of these comments?

. . . .

. . . .

Summarise these comments in your own words:

. . . .

. . . .

. . . .

. . . .

. . . .

CHECKLIST
English essay ✔
Van Gogh notes
Research Genetics
for General Studies
Read Othello 3 iii ✔
Watch 'What the
Papers Say'
(Channel 4, Thursday
9pm)

RECORD SHEET

Study week planner 2: A future model for study

	7-9am	9-11am	11am-1pm	1-3pm	3-5pm	5-7pm	7-9pm	9-11pm
SAT								
SUN								

	7-9am	9am-3pm		3-5pm	5-7pm	7-9pm	9-11pm
MON		Attending					
TUE							
WED							
THU							
FRI							

5 Where to study

Study the four sketches. List the most important advantages and disadvantages of each place of study.

Advantages

. . . .
. . . .
. . . .
. . . .
. . . .

Disadvantages

. . . .
. . . .
. . . .
. . . .
. . . .

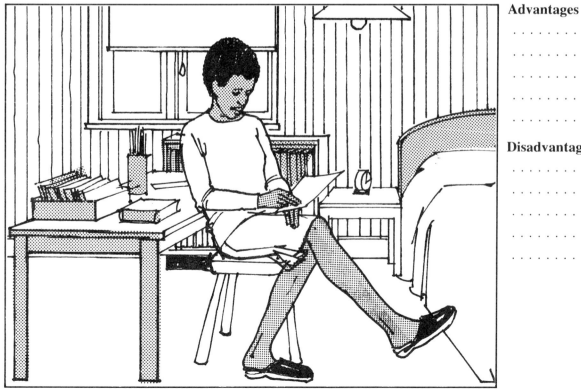

Advantages

. . . .
. . . .
. . . .
. . . .
. . . .

Disadvantages

. . . .
. . . .
. . . .
. . . .
. . . .

Advantages

. . . .
. . . .
. . . .
. . . .
. . . .

Disadvantages

. . . .
. . . .
. . . .
. . . .
. . . .

Advantages

. . . .
. . . .
. . . .
. . . .
. . . .

Disadvantages

. . . .
. . . .
. . . .
. . . .
. . . .

Think about the changes you intend to
make to your place of study.

6 Getting set for study

'
Get up telling yourself you're going to enjoy the day.

Think about what you hope to achieve.

A bit of well earned praise works wonders.
'

Are you ready for success?

A strong, positive view of your studies and your chances of success will be a dominant factor in fulfilling your goals. Your hopes control a mental framework which remains with you whenever you study. Positive thinkers have a stronger framework to support them when they work. Students who are optimistic about their future and their ability to overcome the next hurdle in their study will be more aware of their strengths than their weaknesses. Appreciating your strengths will lead to greater confidence and then further success.

Of course everyone makes mistakes, but learning from mistakes is essential. A confident learner will face those mistakes and use them more effectively than someone who becomes depressed by them and feels all effort to be worthless.

Mental images

You can learn how to develop a strong mental image of yourself and your chances of success by:

1 Studying how other people prepare themselves
2 Organising your study method

You will have noticed how persistent and widespread your mental awareness is after you have bought a distinctive item, for example an article of clothing or a car. You begin to notice all the similar items owned by other people. Every other car is a Metro, every other person is wearing your style or colour of coat. Psychologists call this mental orientation *set*.

Sports people will call it 'psyching'. Watch a highjumper or weightlifter before they perform. Consider what goes through the mind of a tennis player during a break. Before a boxing match, what purpose do the hateful stare and verbal aggression serve?

To have the confidence to score a goal, to believe you can score a goal, indeed, to have a mental picture of yourself scoring a goal, is a key preparation if you take your sport seriously. Imagine your chances of success if you started a race convinced you would come last!

Some mental barriers have proved very difficult to overcome.

The Four Minute Mile Barrier

Before the four minute record for running the mile was broken, times were steadily improving:

1913	Jones	4 mins 14 secs
1915	Taber	4 mins 12.6 secs
1923	Nurmi	4 mins 10.4 secs
1931	Ladoumègue	4 mins 9.2 secs
1933	Lovelock	4 mins 7.6 secs
1934	Cunning	4 mins 6.8 secs
1937	Wooderson	4 mins 6.4 secs
1942	Haag	4 mins 6.2 secs
1942	Anderson	4 mins 6.2 secs
1942	Haag	4 mins 4.6 secs
1943	Anderson	4 mins 2.6 secs
1944	Anderson	4 mins 1.6 secs
1945	Haag	4 mins 1.3 secs

But it was another nine years before the four minute barrier was broken. Could it have been that nobody believed it could be done?

| 1954 | Bannister | 3 mins 59.4 secs |

A very short time after Bannister's record was set, Landy broke it:

| 1954 | Landy | 3 mins 58 secs |

In 1955 Tabori, Chataway and Hewson all ran the mile in less than four minutes in one race! It seems a barrier had been removed.

The present record is:

| 1981 | Coe | 3 mins 48.5 secs |

● A Russian weightlifter only broke the 500lb barrier after the scales had been rigged to show 499lb. Others have broken his record since.

Russian weightlifter Alexev at the Mexico Olympics.

● In the 1968 Mexico Olympics, Bob Beoman, an American long jumper, cleared 8.90 metres (29ft 2½ inches). This broke the world record by 21½ inches. Since then Bob Beoman's record has not been beaten. In fact there have been only small improvements made on the previous world record which Beoman broke. For example Robinson jumped 27 feet 4¾ inches in 1976.

Is a mental barrier developing?

In education it is acknowledged that if a class of pupils believe that they are not very bright, perhaps because they are assigned the title 'set 4' or 'bottom stream', they will work at this level. As these pupils work their mental set makes them more aware of their failures than their successes. It might be the case that their teacher, knowing they are set 4, will look for a set 4 standard because of her or his own mental set.

> Mental set can be positive or negative

Consider the influence of parents, who believe their child to be bright, on the child's own opinion. Think of the opposite case. If two children from different backgrounds, with varying parental expectations, are equally intelligent, which one is more likely to succeed?

> How can we use this very strong mental attitude to our best advantage in study?

● You must have a clear view of your goals

● You must know your long term purpose

● You must recognise the smaller, intermediate steps on the way to your long term goal

Imagine being interviewed by someone who doesn't know you. The interviewer is trying to find out **why you are studying your course.**

Read the questions below then answer them aloud, perhaps you can record your answer and then play them back afterwards.

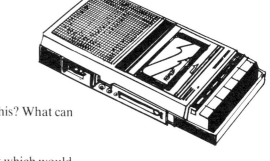

1   What course are you studying, where and to what level?
2   How far through the course are you? How long does it last?
3   How are you getting on? Tell me about your most successful work.
4   Where are you concentrating most of your efforts at the moment?
5   Are you up to date with your work? What is your next task?
6   Is there a work experience element to your course?
7   When are your final exams? What form do the exams take?
8   What use do you hope to make of the qualifications you receive?
9   What are your career ambitions?
10 Which question(s) have you found most difficult to answer? Why is this? What can you do about it?

Work out a question about your goals which you have not been asked but which would have posed problems or even embarrassed you if this interview had been real.

. . . .

. . . .

. . . .

Set for study

 When doing homework that is fairly easy, music helps me to concentrate, but harder homework demands silence.

 Make a list of the other things you have to do, e.g. ring friends, ironing, etc., and do them after studying.

It is useful to have a clear idea of what you hope to achieve in each study session: this clarifies your thoughts and prepares your mental set. By listing what you intend to do you put yourself in the right frame of mind, and are therefore less likely to be distracted.

7 Your body and your brain

Mental abilities do not decline with age

It is important to appreciate this since mature students could hardly expect high quality work if their mental powers are forever decreasing. The decline in the number of brain cells is insignificant compared to the vast number present. No theory of decline in mental abilities up to the age of 60 has been substantiated; in IQ tests no general fall in performance with age has been found. The brain and the thinking process become more specialised as more and more connections are made between brain cells. Experienced learners develop a more complex network of pathways through their brain cells.

In experiments on the protein content of brains of different ages it has been shown that protein levels increase with age. This is consistent with the idea of a chemical basis for memory and a steady increase in mental powers. Why then do some older people claim to be suffering from a declining memory? There are many reasons why a person of any age would claim this to be true, these reasons are examined on page 32.

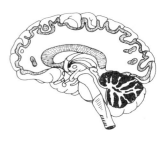

For a more detailed description of the brain and its function see pages 113-115

The things that people do remember most easily are outstanding things. These events are more likely to be outstanding early in our lives rather than later. We become familiar with the way things are in life; what is very unusual or special to a younger person will not be quite so special and memorable to a forty year old.

A healthy brain

The brain requires 25% of our oxygen intake. The blood carrying this oxygen to the brain arrives via tubes of ever decreasing size until it reaches the capillaries in the cortex (see pages 113-115). As we get older these tubes stiffen, the apertures become 'silted up' with materials precipitating from the blood. Excessive intake of cholesterol, in foods containing animal fat, accelerates this deposition. It is likely that this process affects the circulation of the blood and can lead to the heart pumping at higher pressures. The supply of blood to the brain can be affected and there could be a reduction in mental effectiveness.

Take regular exercise

Exercise of the heart, lungs and blood system ensures a good, consistent supply of oxygen to the brain. Most people experience a strong feeling of well-being after exercise. Exercise relieves stress and improves circulation, leading to better mental performance. Students who take regular exercise do better than their sedentary colleagues.

Careful management of your brain means using it well and often. The richer the environment, the more stimulating conversations, pastimes and entertainments you indulge in, the more effective your brain will be. People who have continued working into their eighties and nineties have shown little decline in their powers of observation, analysis and imagination.

Rest

During sleep the proteins which have been used up in the course of the day's mental activities are replenished. The brain can control the amount of sleep you require but steady erosion of this requirement has serious implications for mental awareness and leads to stressful working. You should be aware of the amount of sleep which seems to be right for you and make sure you manage at least that much.

Pacing your study

When you begin to study, the level of electrical activity within your brain rises. As some piece of new information is assimilated new electrical pathways through the brain cells are forged. The new pathways overlap with the pathways from older but similar ideas and information. These processes take time but the more pronounced they are the more likely you are to remember the information later.

Chester: a study example

Imagine you are studying the history of the city of Chester. You would like to remember as much as possible about the city, and particularly its development since Roman times. Study the following passage. Ignore the footnote marks until you have completed your study.

Chester

There have been three phases in the growth of the city of Chester: Roman, medieval and modern. The Roman design of the city, its geographical location at the lowest bridging point on the River Dee, and its position on trading routes, all play a part throughout Chester's history. *A

Roman Chester

Caerleon, York and Chester were the great legionary fortresses which defended the frontiers of Roman Britain. Chester's fortress was built in AD 100-110 out of stone but was previously of wooden construction with an earthwork bank for further protection.

The plan below shows the usual layout of fortresses of this size; access was from each side and the headquarters were central. Barracks, granaries and a hospital were inside the walls; an amphitheatre and civil dwellings were outside the fortified walls. The fortress area is shaded in the plan of Roman and medieval Chester on page 24. *B

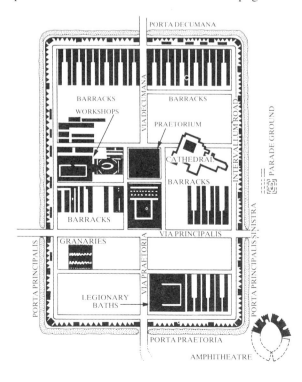

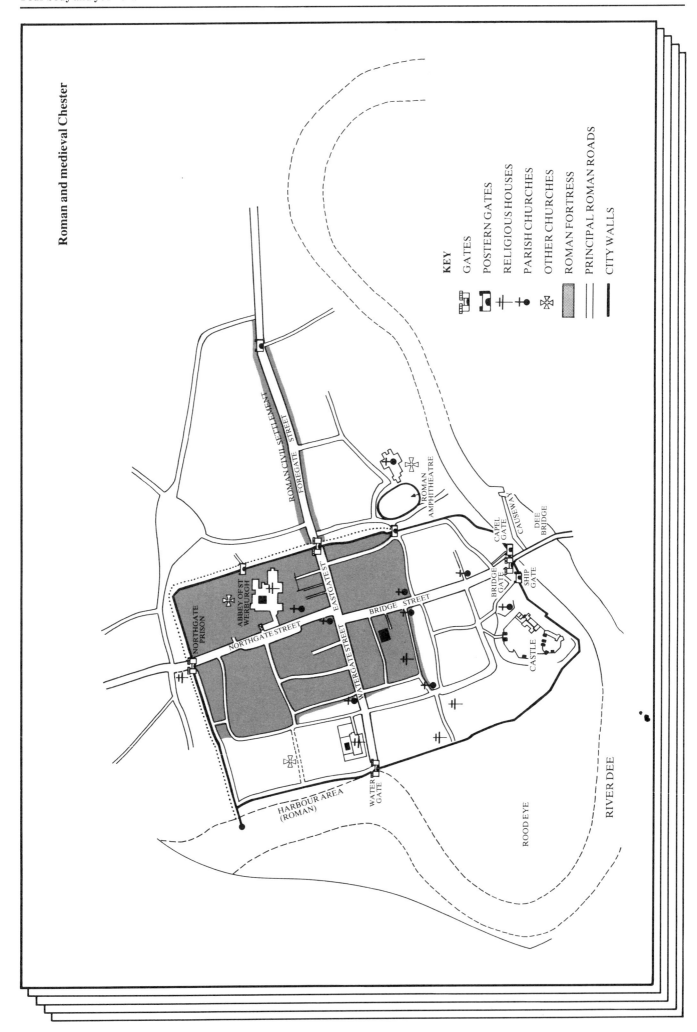

Roman and medieval Chester

KEY

GATES

POSTERN GATES

RELIGIOUS HOUSES

PARISH CHURCHES

OTHER CHURCHES

ROMAN FORTRESS

PRINCIPAL ROMAN ROADS

CITY WALLS

ROMAN CIVIL SETTLEMENT

FOREGATE STREET

ROMAN AMPHITHEATRE

NORTHGATE PRISON

ABBEY OF ST WERBURGH

EASTGATE ST

NORTHGATE STREET

BRIDGE STREET

WATERGATE STREET

CAPEL GATE

CAUSEWAY

DEE BRIDGE

BRIDGE GATE

SHIP GATE

CASTLE

WATER GATE

HARBOUR AREA (ROMAN)

ROOD EYE

RIVER DEE

Medieval Chester

In the tenth century Chester was rebuilt by the Saxons and it became a major trading centre. The Normans established Chester as the centre of an earldom; it was in fact a buffer for attacks against the Welsh. Henry III, however, made the region a royal earldom in 1254 and it was used by Edward I as a base for attacks against the Welsh. By 1284 English rule throughout North Wales was established, and the strategic usefulness of Chester diminished.

In the late fourteenth century Chester became valued as a port, particularly as the embarkation point for troops travelling to Ireland. Alongside Bristol it was the most important western port at this time. It is a coincidence that both these ports have declined through silting up of their estuaries. Chester was probably not appreciably silted until the fifteenth century.*[C]

The principle features of Chester at this time are shown on the map. Notice how the walls built by the Romans have been extended.*[D] The Abbey of St Werbergh was rebuilt during the thirteenth and fourteenth centuries and pressure on space within the walls must have been considerable. There was housing in Foregate Street and beyond Northgate. To the south there was possibly some settlement in Handbridge. The mayor of Chester had rights over the estuary as far as Hoylake and it is likely there were settlements along the course of the river as far as Hoylake.*[E]

Modern Chester

A new quay built at Neston, further up the Dee estuary, revived Chester's shipping trade in the late sixteenth century. But the city's fortunes were low at this time.

Many people died with the outbreak of plague, and their livestock perished in the floods. By 1740 another attempt had been made to invigorate the shipping trade by cutting a passage through the choking Dee sands. New housing and work facilities were built to accommodate the workforce for the new docks. In the late eighteenth century Chester was linked to Nantwich and the Mersey by canals. The canal followed the walls to the north and east. Some industry grew up on the banks of the canal but it was the arrival of the railway link from Crewe to Birkenhead that brought a great increase in activity in the area. With the building of new roads to service the city and public markets, Chester thrived. Many new residential suburbs were established in the nineteenth century.

Although today Chester remains the administrative centre for Cheshire, it has been overtaken in size by towns closer to the vast chemical works which have grown up on Cheshire's salt. All year round Chester is visited by international tourists ready to appreciate the heritage and beauty of the city.*[F]

Now consider the points marked by footnotes:

A It is important to pause here to appreciate these underlying forces in the development of Chester. Moving on too quickly will make the rest of the text appear to be a list of facts and dates without any linking themes. This makes it difficult to understand and remember.

The first paragraph tells you
1 There are three main stages in development of the city. The structure of the extract will follow these stages.
2 The Roman plan is the fundamental structure and future developments only tinkered with this plan.
3 The city's strategic development and defence are based on its geographical position.

B Look at the layout of the fortress; allow yourself time to appreciate this plan as we already know it to be the most influential plan in the history of Chester. Relate the fortress plan to the map of Roman and Medieval Chester.

C Are you clear why Chester became an important trading centre and why it should become the base for attacks against the Welsh?

D Study the map in detail bearing in mind the key points that have been made so far.

E A short pause to allow an adjustment to the new period of study will pay dividends in improved recall.

F Consider what happens when you have finished. If you move on to another subject for study there has been hardly any time for your brain to process the information on Chester, and to establish its links with other related information. Indeed, if you proceed too quickly, then new ideas will flow onto the information about Chester. In this way there is interference which reduces recall later on. If a few minutes rest were taken after your period of study a remarkable increase in appreciation of the study material occurs.

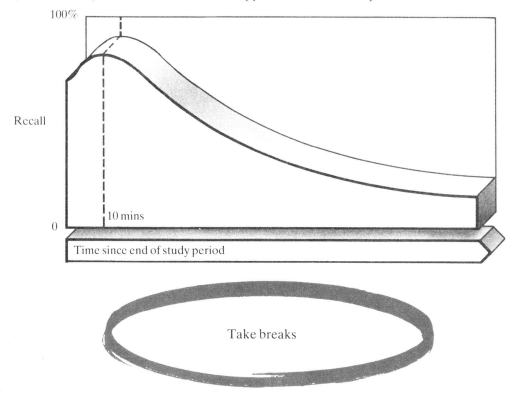

How often you take breaks depends on what you are studying. Routine arithmetic would require few breaks, say every 40 to 60 minutes. Studying a scientific concept or analysing a novel will require more breaks. After 20 minutes most people benefit from a short rest.

You will find that planning your study periods in this way will make your work more satisfying and give you a better appreciation of what you have achieved.

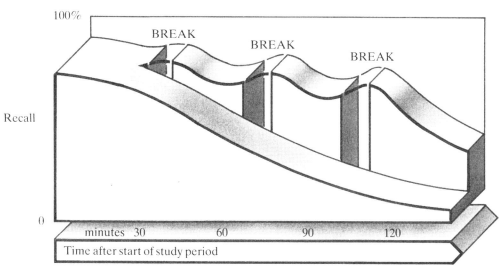

Beware of the temptation to continue without a break, sometimes the urge to keep going can be strong and easily rationalised. During a break try:

1 Moving away from your place of work
2 Taking some fresh air
3 Doing something routine
4 Letting you mind wander off the topic under study
5 Allowing yourself to relax

8 Studying

' *Don't struggle with a topic you don't understand, ask a friend or your teacher.* '

' *Improving your chances of remembering means making the strongest impression possible of the work on your brain.* '

' *Go over your notes now and again. It really helps you to remember them.* '

Study your study

Your place of work should support your studies. For example it should have easy access to files, writing equipment and books for reference. It should be pleasant and interesting but away from distractions. Radio, television and conversation will demand your attention and break your train of thought.

Plan your work

Your work should be planned. You should have a clear idea of the purpose of your study, see pages 18 to 21. Planning evens out your work load and avoids overwork at key times. A steady work rate gives you time to reflect on what you have learnt and allows you to plan a pattern of review times, see page 31. An important aspect of planning is producing a mental set, see page 21. Similarly, checking how you are doing with teachers, lecturers and tutors will lead to greater motivation and better study.

Take breaks

Breaks allow a full processing of information and improve recall, see page 27.

Present your work in a memorable way

Try to ensure that the material you are learning is presented in an interesting, even striking, way. You can make your notes much more memorable by:

1 Organising them well, using sub-headings and showing links between different sections.
2 Designing them in a way which suits the mental processing which will follow. Make them clear, colourful and interesting, see *Making notes*, page 35. Pattern notes are a very useful variation.

Link ideas

It is probable that our memories work by using extensive networks of brain cells. Each idea has its own pattern of cells but some ideas will have common cells in their patterns. You should be able to exploit this association to help you remember.

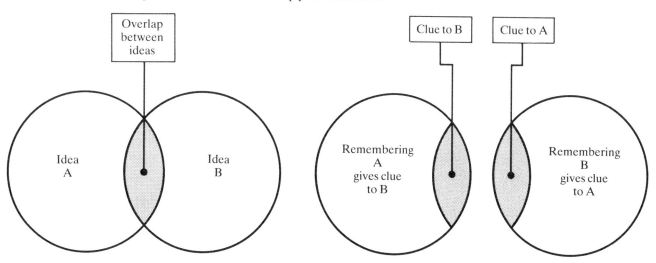

If you can forge links between well established ideas and new ones then both the associated ideas become more strongly recorded in your memory. Give yourself time to appreciate how new ideas and existing ideas can be linked.

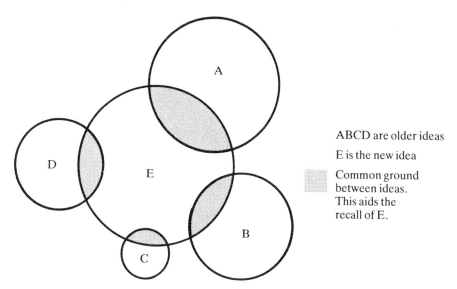

ABCD are older ideas

E is the new idea

Common ground between ideas. This aids the recall of E.

Look back at *Chester*, page 23, and write down two firm links which you made between what you were reading and some information you already knew.

1 New information:

. . . .

. . . .

Existing knowledge:

. . . .

. . . .

2 New information:

. . . .

. . . .

Existing knowledge:

. . . .

. . . .

Do the same for one link established when you looked at the map.

New information:

. . . .

. . . .

Existing knowledge:

. . . .

. . . .

Note down two points made in this book so far that have made a strong impression on your thinking.

1 . . . .

. . . .

2 . . . .

. . . .

Are these closely linked to your experiences?

. . . .

. . . .

Use your knowledge

Using new information or ideas strengthens the mental trace in your brain. Some ideas are readily applied to everyday life. For example, a science student who had just learned about the kinetic theory and the structure of substances, might think through the theory when boiling a kettle. Ideas which are difficult to associate with everyday events can be practised in some artificial way. For example, never underestimate the value of questions: pay serious attention to questions and exercises that demand the use of newly learned information; do this by . . .

● Recognising the point of the question
● Researching the information required
● Designing a solution or answer
● Presenting the solution or answer
● Appreciating what you are learning
● Assessing your performance in answering the question

Answer this question on the history of Chester.

Why was the River Dee such an important influence on
a the early development of the city?
b the prosperity of the city?

Use the six point strategy above to get the most from the exercise.

Teachers use questions as the first structured opportunity for students to review their notes.

Review your work

All newly learned information enters our short term memory. Unless the information is strongly associated with existing knowledge, or proves useful quickly, then it will be forgotten.

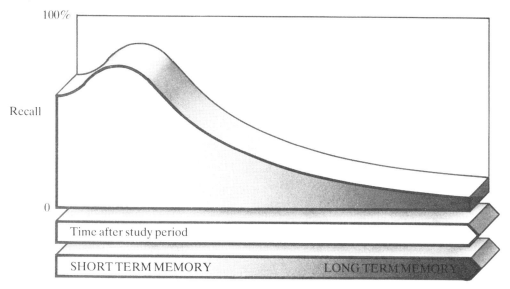

The long term memory develops as associations are appreciated either consciously or subconsciously in the days and nights that follow learning.

Recall improves immediately after learning stops. We can use this fact to improve our chances of remembering.

When a study session is finished it is worth taking a short break and then briefly going over the work again. This review means
1 Looking at the main points again
2 Following the logical progression of ideas
3 Studying your conclusions once more

The Forgetting Curve now takes this shape:

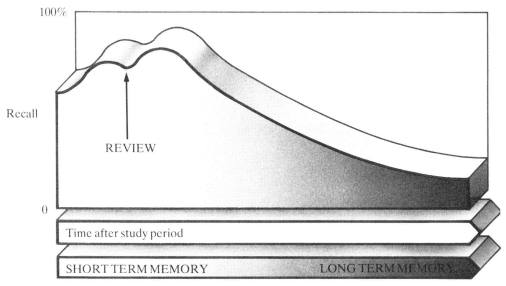

Notice how much more information is consolidated in the long term memory. Further reviews at intervals of a day, a week, a month and three months have a tremendous effect on the amount of information maintained in the long term memory.

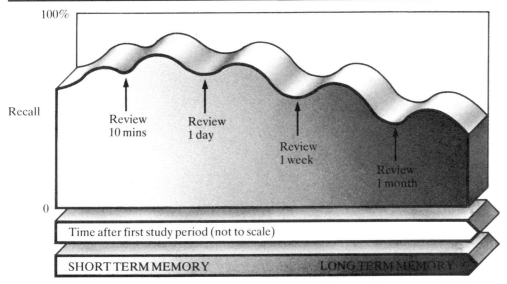

Reviewing and thoughtful note-making can have very significant effects on recall. Most students, however, do not review, because it requires organisation. Every day we would have to review yesterday's notes, and know what other notes to review. By using the pull-out *Study year planner* (in Chapter 4 of the book), however, and by making effective and memorable notes, only a few minutes will be required daily. In comparison to the hours you spend in study, a few minutes spent reviewing is an excellent investment.

Why do we forget?

Consider the theory that memory involves two stages:

Stage 1 Electrical activity which links up a network of brain cells, followed by
Stage 2 Chemical changes in the brain cells which make a more permanent memory trace.

The first stage is temporary and is therefore vulnerable. Reviewing can strengthen the electrical pathways and lead to a more accurate permanent memory. Without reviewing, the natural process of decay will reduce the chances of the second stage occurring. When this happens we forget things, and remember other things inaccurately.

We never learn things in isolation. During a study period new ideas overlap and interconnect with other existing ideas. If there is a weakness in a group of ideas, a misunderstanding or a misconception can spread to the associated ideas and weaken the chance of recalling them. For this reason, notes that you make should be accurate and, if necessary, quite detailed to avoid confusion.

Summary

Mental set can have a decisive influence on the quality of learning. When circumstances are right, when our mind is orientated towards a particular area of study, we can recall more. Reviewing work done in the previous session is an important starting point for study and should be built into your plans.

Surveying your plans will also pay dividends by creating a positive mental set. This is particularly important before examinations.

Study year planner

MARCH	
1	1
2 2nd review of notes on heat	2
3 chem. test.	3
4	4
5 3rd review of calculus notes	5
6	6

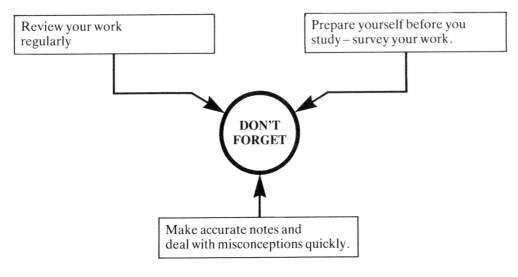

Your body and your brain

PREPARE YOURSELF

KNOW YOUR

STUDY WEEK PLANNER

SET

STUDY STUDY BREAK

SURVEY BEFORE YOU START

WORDS

USE YOUR EFFECTIVELY

ACCURATE NOTES

SHORT TERM MEMORY

KEEP FIT

STUDY YEAR PLANNER

REVIEW

REST

LONG TERM MEMORY

RECORD SHEET

Study profile: A self assessment

Term _____ 198__

Regular reviewing of your progress will

★ keep you up to date   ★ raise your standards   ★ identify areas of concern   ★ build on your strengths   ★ demonstrate your progress

Checklist   **Subject**   **Using the Checklist, comment on your progress. Be honest and realistic**

● achieving potential

● notes up-to-date

● homework done thoroughly

● acting on teachers' advice

● recommended reading

● practical reports up-to-date

● understanding of topics

● suitable notes for reviewing & revision

● background reading

● using resources appropriately

● interest and satisfaction

9 Making notes

' *Make brief memory-jogging notes which can be expanded in essays.* '

' *Write notes in point form with separate sub headings. I find this much easier than revising from long paragraphs and essays.* '

' *Be concise – don't write down everything, as teachers always repeat themselves.* '

' *Concentrate on the relevant points only.* '

Compare these notes

Compare the following two pages of notes about Shakespeare's Theatre. List the most effective notemaking techniques, for example

Craig has simply copied; Carol has reorganised the information. . . . .

. . . .

. . . .

. . . .

. . . .

Which set of notes would be most useful if you had to write an essay on this subject in an exam?

. . . .

. . . .

Which are your notes most like?

. . . .

. . . .

Shakespeare's Theatre

Craig S.

In 1598 the Globe theatre was built from the timbers of a dismantled playhouse called 'The Theatre'. The Globe was built by a theatre company called 'The Lord Chamberlain's Men' – Shakespeare was an important shareholder. Shakespeare was both an actor and a dramatist for the company: all his plays written from 1599 were performed at the Globe.

The Globe was burnt down on the 29 June 1613 during a performance of Henry VIII. A new Globe, with tiling instead of thatching, was built and opened on the 30 June 1614. The Globe was pulled down in 1644.

Performances were given during the afternoon. The auditorium was uncovered and surrounded the stage on three sides. People who stood here were called 'groundlings' – they paid 1d to get in. There were also three galleries. Members of the audience who sat on the stage itself were called 'gallants'. The Globe could hold up to 3,000 people.

Shakespeare's Plays

1590-91 Henry VI (3 parts)	1596 King John	1603 All's well that ends well
1592 Richard III	1597 The Merchant of Venice	Measure for Measure
Titus Andronicus	Henry IV Part 1	1604 Othello
1593 The Comedy of Errors	1598 Henry IV Part 2	1605 Timon of Athens
The Taming of the Shrew	The Merry Wives of Windsor	1606 King Lear
1594 Two Gentlemen of Verona	1599 Henry V	Macbeth
Love's Labour's Lost	Much Ado About Nothing	1607 Antony + Cleopatra
1595 Romeo and Juliet	Julius Caesar	Coriolanus
Richard II	1600 As You Like It	1609 Cymbeline
1596 A Midsummer Night's Dream	Twelfth Night	1610 The Winter's Tale
	1601 Hamlet	1611 The Tempest
	1602 Troilus and Cressida	1612 Henry VIII

SHAKESPEARE'S THEATRE   Carol A.

1. (groundlings)

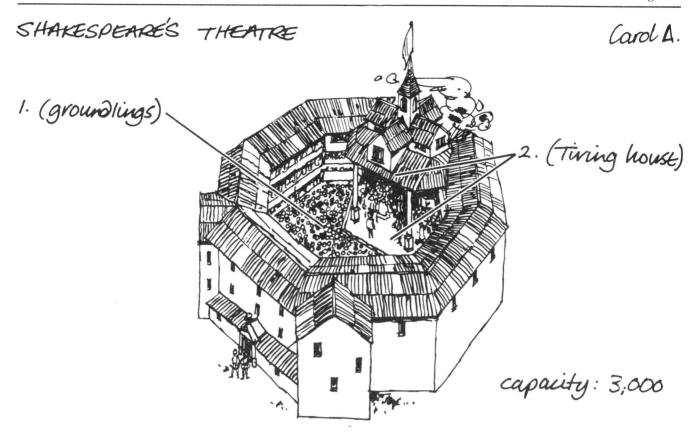

2. (Tiring house)

capacity: 3,000

DEVELOPMENT • Pre 1575 no theatres. Performances: court, houses, halls, open air.
• 1575 – 1616 12 public theatres est in London (pop 200,000)
• 1598 Globe built by Lord Chamberlain's Men. Sh. a major shareholder.

ELIZABETHAN THEATRE

1. Audience surround stage on 3 sides
   Daylight performance
   Mainly standing audience

2. Almost no scenery, no curtain
   No consistency in use of costume
   Soliloquy; blank verse; boy
   actors as women (till 1660)

3. Doesn't confuse illusion with
   reality) ∴ encourages critical
   scrutiny, as well as enjoyment,
   of characters, themes + play.

MODERN THEATRE UP TO 1960

Audience face proscenium arch.
Sophisticated lighting.
Seated audience.

Realistic scenery, stage curtain.
Historically accurate costume
Use of realistic effects
Believable casting.

Encourages dramatic illusion.
Usually aims to be realistic and
credible. A character's, not an
actor's, stage.

Why make notes?

All students make notes but most do this without really thinking about *why* they are
making them. Why should you make notes?

. . . .

. . . .

. . . .

. . . .

. . . .

1 Making notes makes you concentrate on what you are learning.
2 Notes help you understand because you put ideas into your own words and diagrams.
3 Notes link new knowledge to what you already know.
4 On paper it is easier to distinguish between important points and supporting details.
5 Notes are excellent for revision.
6 You remember things better when you have noted them down.

Copied and dictated notes

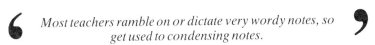

> *Dictation goes through your ears, down your arm and onto
> the paper without stopping in the brain in between.*

> *Most teachers ramble on or dictate very wordy notes, so
> get used to condensing notes.*

Notes which have been copied or dictated are a poor aid to understanding because you
have missed the vital stage of interpreting the information for yourself. Therefore make
sure you have understood what you've heard or read before you start to make your own
notes.

Key words

> *Try to sum up sentences in one word, which is the key
> word of the sentence and should remind you of the rest
> of the sentence.*

Key words are the ones which are most loaded with meaning, the ones that unlock your
memory. Key words are mostly nouns and verbs.

Read this article to discover what is the government's attitude to the health risks of lead
in petrol. Underline the key words which describe the Government's attitude.

How they stall on lead

by Des Wilson

(This is a shortened version of an article that appeared in *The Guardian* on 29.7.82)

IT IS difficult to say what is more disturbing – the firm scientific evidence that children are at serious risk of neurological dysfunction caused by pollution from lead in petrol, or the chilling cynicism of Ministers and civil servants in defence of their refusal to ban it.

Whitehall has specially created a defensive mechanism on the subject. No matter whether you write to the Ministers responsible for Health, Transport, Energy, or Environmental matters, you receive almost exactly the same reply. So far they have adopted the following evasive, prevaricative, or, to put it mildly, less than truthful devices to counter ever-increasing public unrest on the issue:

"In our view, none of the recent evidence adds significantly to the information available to us when we made the decision . . . announced last May (1981)." (Giles Shaw, 25/3/82; Lynda Chalker, 22/4/82).

Incorrect. There have been eight major items of evidence associating lead with neurological dysfunction since Ministers took their decision on the basis of the Lawther Committee report Lead and Health, and none are consistent with Lawther's conclusions.

That is why Professor Michael Rutter, a member of that committee, and one of the world's leading child psychiatrists, reviewing the up-to-date evidence, recently stated: "The best of the most recent studies have indeed failed to disprove the hypothesis that low-level lead exposure leads to psychological impairment . . . the implication is that it would be both safer in practice and scientifically more appropriate to act as if the hypothesis were true rather than to continue to act as if it were untrue."

That is why the British Medical Association has recently concluded that "associations have been demonstrated between impairment in mental functioning and lead levels below the range previously considered harmful. At first there was some doubt about the validity of these studies but it is now generally accepted that the association is real and it should not therefore be disregarded."

These two objective and widely-respected sources of opinion have no political or economic interest in the issue.

"The British Medical Association's evidence to the Royal Commission on Environmental pollution . . . is a balanced document reaching similar conclusions to those reached a year ago by the Government. . . . I welcome it as a reinforcement of the Government's views." (Kenneth Clarke 20/5/82).

A complete distortion of the position: the above quotation from the BMA document and two quoted below in this article, reveal an enormous gulf between the BMA and the position of Ministers. The BMA document is a direct challenge to the Government's view.

"There is no convincing evidence that harm is caused at blood lead levels below 35 ug/dl." (Kenneth Clarke 9/7/82).

Incorrect. As the BMA said: "On the basis of the evidence it has received, the BMA considers that lead is capable of causing harm at levels of exposure previously considered safe i.e. at levels indicated by 30 ug/dl" Drs Yule and Lansdown, two Lawther Committee members, revealed an average IQ, deficit in children in London at 13 ug/dl and above. EEG studies from the United States have shown effects on brainwave patterns at 7 ug/dl.

Professor Rutter has said that "the Lawther Committee's suggestion that we know there are no ill effects below 35 ug/dl is wrong." It is known that Ministers have been advised by officials to reduce the safety threshold to 25 ug/dl (still far too high) but resist this because of political implications.

"Taken as a whole, the results
(of an EEC screening of blood lead levels) reinforce the Government's view that levels of lead pollution in the environment give no cause for alarm." (Giles Shaw 30/6/82).

Incorrect. The studies indicated few children with blood lead levels over 35 ug/dl. Good news – if that was a safe level. But, as I have made clear above, this threshold is far too high. A realistic threshold of 10 ug/dl would throw up an entirely different result. It is a classic Governmental device to fix unrealistically high official safety levels so that the majority of people will fall below them, and thus public concern will not be aroused.

* * *

So, what it all adds up to is a sorry tale of Ministers desperately defending the status quo by ignoring the inflowing tide of evidence of both the health hazard and the contribution of petrol lead to overall lead burdens. The horror of the situation is that they care more about saving face than the fact that generations of children are used as guinea pigs.

Des Wilson is the chairman of CLEAR, the Campaign for Lead Free Air, which is based at 2 Northdown Street, London N1.

The headline here is an invitation to read. Write your own headline which summarises the story.

. . . .

. . . .

Sprays

Sprays are a way of quickly jotting down all your ideas on a subject and linking them up. Sprays save time because you don't have to write sentences or put words down in any particular order.

Stage 1: Putting the ideas down

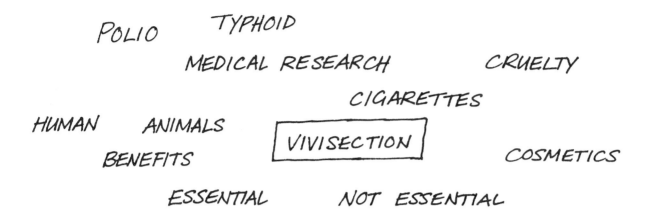

Stage 2: Making the links

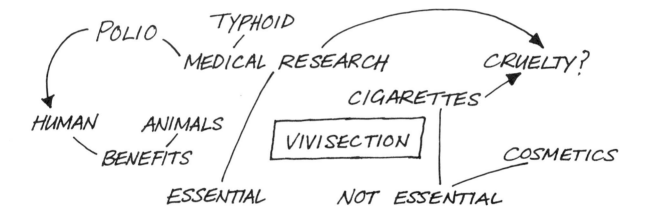

Practise this technique by making a spray about

Visual and pattern notes

One picture is worth a thousand words.

'*Use flow diagrams to explain processes. Diagrams can omit half the written explanation.*'

Pattern notes (sometimes called 'mind maps' or 'concept trees') are a valuable supplement to ordinary written notes (called 'linear notes') because

- One pattern note can sum up many pages of written notes
- They make you concentrate on the fundamentals: the more important, or relevant, an idea is, the closer it will be to the centre of the note
- They help you to see the relationships between different aspects of a subject
- They link existing and new knowledge
- They put a topic into perspective
- Making a pattern note is a very active form of learning
- Every pattern note is different
- Because our visual memory is better than our verbal memory pattern notes are a great aid to recall
- Pattern notes are an effective way of planning an essay
- They are an absorbing and fruitful method of revising
- Pattern notes are flexible because you can easily add to the note later
- You can use the techniques of pattern notes to brighten up your linear notes
- Pattern notes are fun

Look at the flow chart on aluminium, and the pattern note on accent, page 42. Now make your own pattern note or flow chart on a topic. Use colour-coding on related ideas; and print, box or underline headings.

THE EXTRACTION OF ALUMINIUM

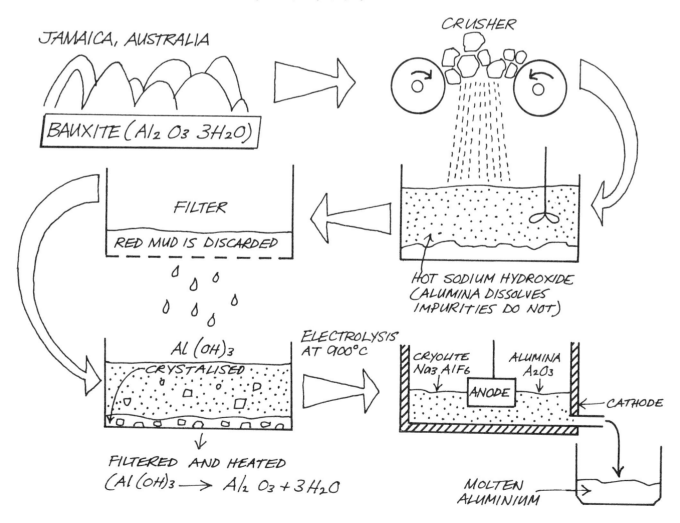

SOCIAL

↓

JUDGEMENTS

ACCORDING
TO →

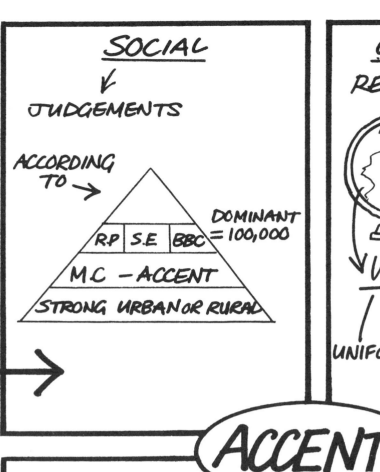

DOMINANT
= 100,000

| R.P | S.E | BBC |

M.C — ACCENT

STRONG URBAN OR RURAL

GEOGRAPHICAL

REGIONAL

GEORDIE

SCOUSE

COCKNEY

PIDGIN

W. INDIAN
ASIAN

↓ USA

INFLUENCES

CITY X

UNIFORMITY

BLACK
EUROPEAN

COUNTRY ✓

ACCENT

CONFORMITY

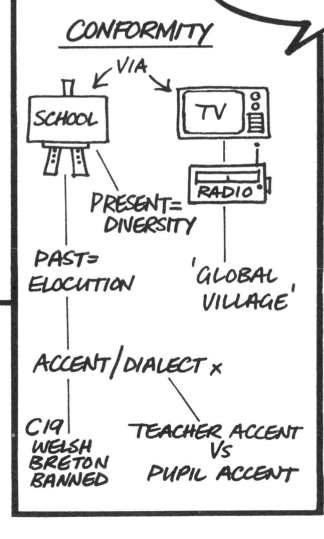

VIA

SCHOOL

TV

RADIO

PRESENT =
DIVERSITY

PAST =
ELOCUTION

'GLOBAL
VILLAGE'

ACCENT / DIALECT x

C19
WELSH
BRETON
BANNED

TEACHER ACCENT
Vs
PUPIL ACCENT

DIALECT

↙ VOCABULARY

snap, butties

GRAMMAR

I and I rule
Fetch us coats
I was stood

PRONUNCIATION

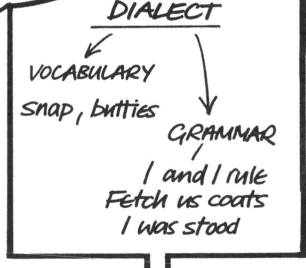

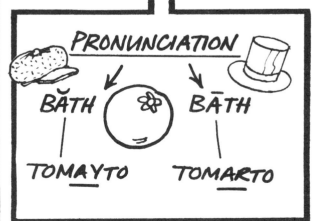

BĂTH

BĀTH

TOMAYTO

TOMARTO

Revising from notes

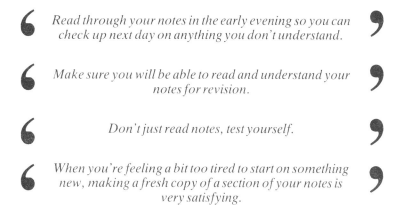

> *Read through your notes in the early evening so you can check up next day on anything you don't understand.*

> *Make sure you will be able to read and understand your notes for revision.*

> *Don't just read notes, test yourself.*

> *When you're feeling a bit too tired to start on something new, making a fresh copy of a section of your notes is very satisfying.*

There are a number of different ways of revising from notes:

1 **Reading notes just before the exam.** If you leave it this late, the sheer bulk of your notes will be daunting. As a result you will feel under stress even before you have begun to revise.

2 **Regular re-reading of notes** one day, one week, one month, three months and then six months after writing them. The pull-out Study Year Planner will help you to organise this. Although this may seem like a lot of work, in fact, it is particularly efficient because your learning is reinforced regularly.

3 **Underlining** key points in red, or with a highlighter pen.

4 **Making a pattern note** to summarise a whole section of notes.

5 **Re-drafting notes in a concise form.** You should write up your notes in best as soon as possible, ideally on the same day. Holidays are an excellent time to rewrite and condense your notes. Record (index) cards (5″ × 3″) are a handy format for this: they are pocket size and you can make use of the odd moment, in the bus queue for example, to revise.

FACT SHEET

Filing notes

It is frustrating and time wasting to have made notes on a subject and then not to be able to find them when you need them. Once you have made your notes you need to keep them in a place that is accessible, and in an order that's easy to follow.

Making notes on file paper, rather than in a book, allows you to add and organize the material. **A4 file paper** is a handy standard size, and is easier to store than the larger foolscap size.

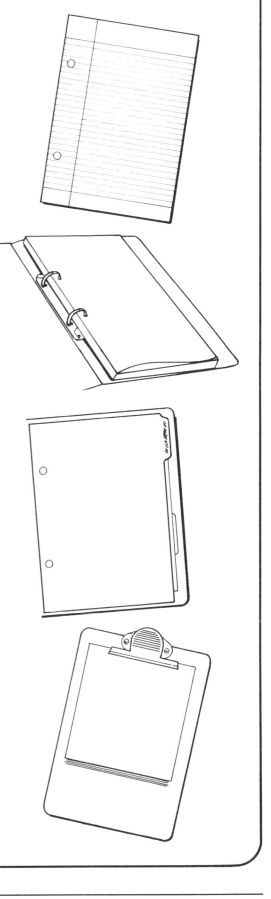

An **A4 Ring Binder** keeps your current notes together and is easy to carry about.

Dividers organize your file. You can buy them or make them yourself.

You don't have to carry your A4 Ring Binder file around – you can keep your immediate notes and handouts on a **clipboard**, and file the others away.

Filing is part of the process of revision because
1   you know where your notes are when you need them
2   deciding where to file your notes means you have to glance at them, and think about what category they belong to. This is a stimulus to your memory.

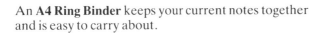

FACT SHEET

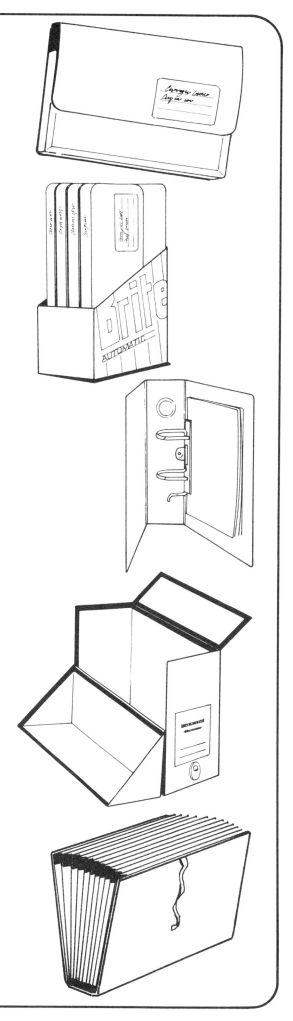

Storing notes

If you have a lot of notes then it is expensive to have to buy more ring binders. Instead you can file the notes which you are not currently using. There are a number of possibilities which are listed below in order of expense, beginning with the cheapest.

Large envelopes are convenient, or you can buy **document wallets** – it is better to buy the slightly more expensive ones which are glued at the sides so that your notes don't fall out. Clear **plastic wallets** are particularly useful because you can see immediately what is inside.

A large (E10) **washing powder box** can be cut to file these wallets of notes.

Lever arch files are a little more expensive than ring binders but can hold 2 or 3 times as many pages. They are not as easy to flick through as the ring binder.

Box files are hard wearing, but, without dividers, notes can be hard to find in them.

Concertina files hold more than the above, and are available in cardboard and metal versions. They allow you to see at a glance where your notes on a topic are. When full they are heavy to move.

FACT SHEET

Storing notes

Record cards are especially useful when you come to revising because they help you to concentrate on the essentials. You can put the chief points about a topic down, almost as if this was a plan for an exam essay. You can then carry the card round in your bag or pocket to revise in odd moments.

Record cards are available in three sizes: 5″ × 3″, 6″ × 4″, and 8″ × 5″. Any card that you are going to use a lot can be covered in clear plastic adhesive. You can file the cards in an old shoe box, with the help of a few dividers. Alternatively you can buy plastic boxes to file them in.

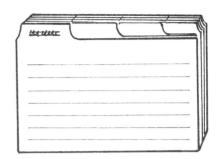

If you have a great number of notes a small **filing cabinet** can be useful. It is possible to buy second-hand cabinets from some office equipment shops.

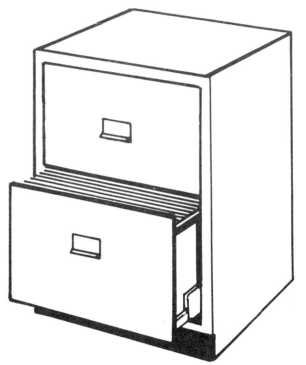

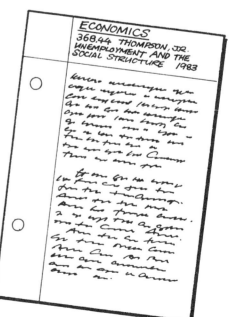

Arranging notes

It is best to arrange your notes thematically according to subject. Don't be afraid to re-arrange them, and sub-divide as themes become clearer during your course of study.

If you have taken notes from several books and articles on a topic you could arrange these notes alphabetically according to title or author. If you have been given a booklist you could note on it where you have filed your notes.

When taking notes from library books don't forget to note the code number, author and title, so you can quickly find the book again if you need it.

10 Abbreviations

Clear and accurate abbreviations are used widely to save time and space when writing notes. In some books and articles the words or phrases which are used frequently are written out at the beginning of the article and then abbreviated afterwards.

Some students write notes with connecting words missing. Save time + space, be careful when reading notes, interpret accurately.

Another method of abbreviating notes is to leave out all the vowels: ths s stll srprsngly smpl t rd.

Match the abbreviations in the boxes below with their corresponding words in the list.

```
∴  %  pp  NB  cf  op  cit
ibid  et al  @  ∴  ie  ♀
min  h  c1475  C19  ♂  "
```

```
m  kg  s  V  °C  Cal  °F
l  Ar  Mr  ρ  log  ≥
>  ln  <  λ  J
```

General abbreviations

female . . . .

minutes . . . .

pages . . . .

therefore . . . .

about . . . .

per cent . . . .

male . . . .

hours . . . .

compare . . . .

at . . . .

because . . . .

in other words . . . .

century . . . .

in the work cited . . . .

and others . . . .

in the same place . . . .

note well . . . .

same as above, ditto . . . .

Scientific abbreviations

less than . . . .

litre . . . .

density . . . .

metre . . . .

logarithm . . . .

calorie . . . .

volt . . . .

degrees Farenheit . . . .

kilogram . . . .

wavelength . . . .

relative atomic mass . . . .

greater than . . . .

natural logarithm . . . .

degrees centigrade . . . .

relative molecular mass . . . .

greater than or equal to . . . .

second . . . .

joule . . . .

Note below any other abbreviations of your own that you are going to use in your work.

11 Library and research skills

' *Ask how the system works because it's difficult at first.* '

' *Compare bookstocks and study facilities at the libraries nearest you.* '

' *Use the same library and try to get to know it.* '

' *Research makes you discover things for yourself, and that's one of the best ways of learning.* '

Choosing a library

A good library will provide you with

- Up-to-date books, magazines, periodicals and other sources on your subject
- Expert advice on how to make the most of the library's facilities
- A quiet and convenient place to work, with an atmosphere that encourages study

It is a sensible idea at the beginning of your course to find out which libraries you can use within a reasonable travelling distance.

Your library

The library which is part of the institution you are studying at will automatically allow you to

- Borrow books
- Study in the library

However the smaller the educational institution the more limited its library services will be in terms of

- An up-to-date and extensive bookstock
- A wide range of reference sources
- Professional advice. Small libraries may be staffed by clerical assistants rather than by professional librarians
- Opening hours

The public library

Branch or central library?
A local branch library may be useful for light reading, and for studying if it has a separate reference section. For serious study and research, however, you will need to go to the central library which will provide separate lending and reference libraries, as well as the sort of studious atmosphere which many students find an aid to self discipline and concentration.

Large libraries also have a photocopier, perhaps teletext, and some even have a cafe.

Membership

If you are studying away from home you will be able to be a member of both your home public library and the public library at your place of study. Similarly if you are not a full time student but work outside the local authority area in which you live then you will be able to join the library service of both authorities. Tickets issued by your local public library can be used in any public library.

When you are applying for membership of a public library take along with you some proof of your identity and address.

A local academic library

It may well be possible to use the library of a local college, polytechnic or university, for study and reference *if* you ask permission. These libraries will not, however, allow you to borrow books.

Getting to know your way round

By getting to know the library you intend to use most, you will

● Feel more at home there
● Be able to locate quickly the books you want
● Be able to settle quickly to your work

Advice

At both large public libraries and college libraries you will be able to obtain expert advice. Look for 'Information' or 'Readers' Adviser' signs, or ask the assistants on the counter to direct you to the professional staff. One of the librarians may have a qualification in your subject.

Guides

Many libraries have some form of printed guide which lists their facilities and services. Some college libraries arrange special introductory sessions and tours for new students.

Library plan

If there is a library plan on display this may reveal less obvious facilities of the library, eg a local history collection, a slide library or a software library.

Browsing

This is an excellent way of getting to know the library, and also makes a break from your studies.

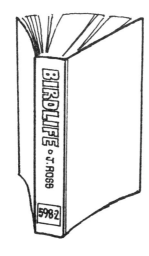

Finding a book

Each subject is given a code, called a classification number, which is put on the spine of the book. Books are arranged by this number on the shelf.

How to find books and information on a subject

To find information on a topic you must first find the code number for that subject. You can find this by looking in the Library Subject Index, which is probably a part of the card catalogue. If there is nothing on your subject it might be listed under a different name. Try thinking of another word, perhaps a more general or more specific term. On the left below, for example, are some headings you might first think of, and on the right are terms that they might be listed under in a subject index

Argon	*see* Rare Gases
Moslem religion	*see* Islam
Smoking	*see* Addiction
Adolescents	*see* Young People
Etchings	*see* Prints
Sexism	*see* Women: Sociology

Because knowledge can't be neatly pigeonholed you'll find the subject index may tell you to look in more than one place, often sending you to a more general, or more specific, heading:

Eustachian tube
        see also Middle ear
Symbolism
        see also specific art forms

FACT SHEET

The library catalogue

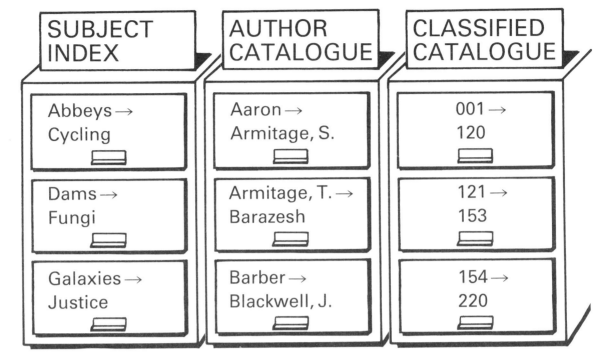

SUBJECT INDEX	AUTHOR CATALOGUE	CLASSIFIED CATALOGUE
Abbeys → Cycling	Aaron → Armitage, S.	001 → 120
Dams → Fungi	Armitage, T. → Barazesh	121 → 153
Galaxies → Justice	Barber → Blackwell, J.	154 → 220

The library catalogues are either drawers containing 5″ × 3″ cards, or are information on microfiche or computer printout. These catalogues often look imposing and off-puting but with very little practice are straightforward to use.

Subject index

This lists alphabetically hundreds of subjects, and gives the library code (classification number) for each. In other words, it tells you where to look in the library, but it doesn't list the books.

Author catalogue

Every book in the library is arranged here in alphabetical order by author's surnames. This also includes editors and the names of committees which have produced reports.

Classified catalogue

All the books in the library are recorded here in numerical order according to their classification number. To use this catalogue you have to first find out from the **Subject index** the number for the subject you are interested in.

Dictionary catalogue

Instead of a classified catalogue some libraries have a dictionary catalogue. This lists all the books in the library in alphabetical order according to their subject.

Title catalogue

Some libraries also have a title catalogue but often this is for fiction books only.

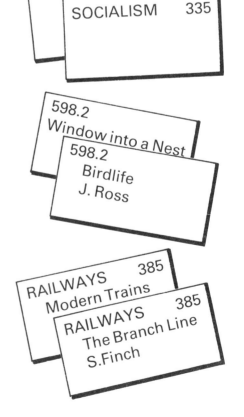

SOILS 631.4

SOCIALISM 335

598.2
Window into a Nest

598.2
Birdlife
J. Ross

RAILWAYS 385
Modern Trains

RAILWAYS 385
The Branch Line
S. Finch

Books on some subjects may be classified under a number of different headings according to the aspect and approach to the topic, for example

Computers:

Accountancy	657
Education	370.778
Graphic Arts	760
Management	658.05
Office Equipment	651.8
Programming	001.642
Social Effects	303.483

In public and many college libraries the Dewey classification is used. This divides knowledge up into ten main divisions. Each main division is then divided into ten major headings, for example Geography and History – the 900s – are divided up in the table below. Each one of these major headings is then divided into ten important subjects, for example the history of modern Europe, 940, is divided up below.

MAIN DIVISIONS		GEOGRAPHY & HISTORY		HISTORY OF MODERN EUROPE	
000	General topics	900	General works	940	General works
100	Philosophy & Psychology	910	Geography	941	Scotland & Ireland
200	Religion	920	Biography	942	England & Wales
300	Social Sciences	930	History of the ancient world	943	Central Europe
400	Languages	940	History of modern Europe	944	France
500	Pure sciences	950	History of modern Asia	945	Italy
600	Technology	960	History of modern Africa	946	Iberian Peninsula
700	The Arts	970	History of North America	947	Eastern Europe
800	Literature	980	History of South America	948	Scandanavia
900	Geography & History	990	History of the rest of the world	949	Other parts of Europe

On the next page is a list of the main headings in the Dewey classification

FACT SHEET

Library classification: The Dewey System

000	GENERAL WORKS
010	Bibliography
020	Librarianship
030	Encyclopedias
070	Journalism
100	PHILOSOPHY
110	Metaphysics
120	Epistemology
130	The paranormal
140	Specific philosophies
150	Psychology
160	Logic
170	Ethics
180	Ancient, medieval & Oriental philosophy
190	Modern western philosophy
200	RELIGION
210	Natural religion
220	The Bible
230	Christian theology
240	Moral theology
250	The local church; religious orders
260	Social theology
270	Church history
280	Christian churches & sects
290	Other religions
300	SOCIAL SCIENCES
310	Statistics
320	Political science
330	Economics
340	Law
350	Public administration
360	Social problems & services
370	Education
380	Commerce
390	Customs, folklore
400	LANGUAGE
410	Linguistics
420	English
430	German
440	French
450	Italian
460	Spanish; Portuguese
470	Latin
480	Clasical Greek
490	Other languages

500	PURE SCIENCES
510	Mathematics
520	Astronomy
530	Physics
540	Chemistry
550	Geology
560	Fossils
570	Anthropology; Biology
580	Botany
590	Zoology
600	TECHNOLOGY
610	Medicine
620	Engineering
630	Agriculture
640	Home economics, housecraft
650	Business & management
660	Chemical technology
670	Manufactures
680	Manufactures for specific purposes
690	Buildings
700	THE ARTS
710	Town & country planning
720	Architecture
730	Sculpture
740	Drawing
750	Painting
760	Graphic arts; prints
770	Photography
780	Music
790	Recreations; theatre & television; sport
800	LITERATURE
810	American
820	English
830	German
840	French
850	Italian
860	Spanish; Portuguese
870	Latin
880	Greek
890	Other literatures
900	GEOGRAPHY & HISTORY
910	Geography; travel
920	Biography
930	Ancient history
940	European history
950	Asian history
960	African history
970	North American history
980	South American history
990	History of other areas

How to find a book if you know the author

Look up the surname in the author catalogue to find the classification number which tells you where the book is shelved.

> MENZEL, Donald Howard   523.2
>
> A Field Guide to the Stars and Planets
> Collins 1977

Some library catalogues are now on microfiche which means that you will have to use a viewer to consult the catalogue.

Many libraries have their books listed in a classified numerical order, according to the library code number, as well as in alphabetical order by the author's surname. You can use the 'classified catalogue' to see what books the library has on your subject, whether they are reference, lending, reserve stock, special collection, pamphlet or whatever. For the ordinary student this is not as useful as scanning the shelves and examining the books themselves, but it is valuable for those doing original research.

How to find a book if you know only its title

If the book is in print (i.e. it is still being sold) then look up the title in *British Books in Print*, or if it is a brand new book look it up in the monthly updated microfiche version of British Books in Print, and this will tell you the author. If the book is out of print it is best to ask a librarian. Remember the librarians are there to help you.

If the library has the book but you can't find it

If another reader has it then you can reserve the book for a small fee, but this might mean waiting several weeks – so plan well ahead. Otherwise the book may be shelved elsewhere, perhaps in the Reference library, in a short loan collection kept behind the counter, or in Reserve Stock, so check the catalogue again.

If the library doesn't have the book you want

You can ask the librarian to obtain it for you. Fill in a card giving as many details about the book as you can (author, title, date of publication, where you saw the book reviewed or mentioned). The librarian will decide to either purchase the book or borrow it through the *Inter Library Loan System*. In either case it will take quite a few weeks to come. You should tell the librarian if you have a deadline for using the book – it may not be possible to obtain the book as quickly as you need it.

Remember the books you need may be in demand so plan well ahead.

12 Key reference books explained

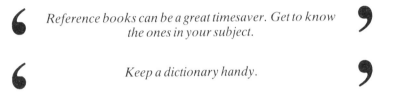

' *Reference books can be a great timesaver. Get to know the ones in your subject.* '

' *Keep a dictionary handy.* '

Some of these books will be found in all libraries. Larger libraries should have them all in the latest edition.

General

British National Bibliography (BNB)   This weekly publication lists all the new books published in the UK. There is a monthly index, and a four monthly and annual cumulation. There are two annual volumes, one listing all the books in the last year in classified Dewey order (see Library & research skills page 50), while the other volume contains an author and title index giving the Dewey classification number, and an alphabetical list of subjects with their Dewey number. Don't be put off by the long classification numbers that BNB uses.

Guinness Book of Answers   "A handbook of general knowledge" with facts & diagrams on topics from The Calendar to Anthropology. There is a section on Countries, and Counties of the UK.

British Technology Index (BTI)   A monthly index of articles in periodicals in technology arranged by subject with an author index. This is also available on microfilm.

British Humanities Index   A similar index to BTI (above) indexing periodicals in the humanities.

Dictionaries

Collins English Dictionary   This is the best one volume English dictionary. It was published in 1979 and has 162,000 references, with a single A-Z listing for all terms including abbreviations, and some 14,000 biographical and geographical entries. Its coverage of scientific terms is unrivalled. Unlike the *Oxford English Dictionary* definitions are arranged so that the modern meaning of a word is given first.

Oxford English Dictionary (OED)   12 volumes, 1933. Work originally began on the dictionary in the late nineteenth century. Four supplementary volumes are being published to bring the dictionary up-to-date. About 415,000 words are defined, the definitions of each word being given in historical order of meaning. Thus the most recent meanings are given last. In other words the dictionary is organised on historical principles. Quotations are used to illustrate the definitions. A microprint two volume edition entitled *The Compact Oxford English Dictionary* was published in 1971 and comes complete with a magnifying glass.

The Oxford Dictionary of Quotations gives more than 40,000 quotes arranged according to author. There is a key word index of some 70,000 terms.

Encyclopedias

Encyclopedia Britannica (USA)   The latest edition (known as 'Britannica 3') is divided, confusingly, into three sections:
Propaedia: an outline of knowledge, and a guide to the Britannica itself.
Micropedia: 10 volumes of short articles for ready reference.
Macropaedia: 19 volumes of long scholarly articles

World Book Encyclopedia (USA)   This 22 volume work is the best encyclopedia for school use. Volumes 23 & 24 are devoted to the British Isles.

Encyclopedia Americana   Arranged in one alphabetical sequence, this is less confusing to use than Britannica.

McGraw-Hill Encyclopedia of Science and Technology (USA) is a scholarly 15 volume encyclopedia, arranged in alphabetical order by subject.

Year Books & Annual Publications

The Statesman's Year Book is a volume of international facts, figures & statistics. Countries are listed alphabetically, and information is arranged under headings such as 'Economy', 'Communications' and 'Natural Resources'. International organisations are also treated.

Whitaker's Almanack   This volume contains a great deal of miscellaneous information.

Pears Cyclopedia   Within the double columned, tightly packed volume, are sections on 'People', 'Ideas & Beliefs', 'Medical Matters', 'Sport' etc. There is a gazetteer and index.

Who's Who contains 26,000 biographies of living people, chiefly British, given in a standard format of name, present position, date of birth, family details, education, career, publications, recreations and address.

Britain: an official handbook "is primarily concerned to describe the machinery of government & other institutions, together with the necessary physical & social background." There are sections on defence, overseas relations, social welfare, justice and so on.

Statistics

Social Trends published annually by the Central Statistical Office, gives detailed statistical charts, tables & information on the UK under headings such as 'Education', 'Employment', 'Leisure' and 'Law Enforcement'. It is about "broad changes in society. It focuses on people rather than institutions . . ."

Annual Abstract of Statistics   This larger volume, also published by the Central Statistical Office, covers all aspects of the economic, social and industrial life in the UK. The tables often give comparative figures over a decade.

Geography

Times Atlas of the World   The five volume edition was produced between 1955 and 1960. A separate Index-Gazetteer was published in 1965. The Comprehensive single volumed edition has an index of some 210,000 names.

Columbia Lippincott Gazetteer of the World (USA) lists in one alphabetical sequence countries, towns, islands, rivers etc., giving such information as population, location, trade, agriculture and communications about each. As an indication of its scope, every village in France with a population of over 2,000 will be listed here.

Other works

Keesing's Contemporary Archives is "a record of national and international current events with continually updated indexes". The information has been taken from the press and broadcasting. It is updated weekly, with outline, names and analytical indexes.

Granger's Index to Poetry (USA) contains a title & first line index, an author index and a subject index. The work indexes 514 volumes of anthologised poetry. The subject index includes nearly 5,000 topics including Women's Liberation.

Roget's Thesaurus is probably more useful than a dictionary when you are writing an essay. If you are at a loss for the exact word, or phrase, you need, then look up any equivalent you can think of in the index. This will then offer you a variety of shades of meaning. Choose the one closest to your requirements, and look up the number beside it in the main text of the thesaurus. Here you will find a keyword, and sub-headings, followed by numerous synonyms.

The New Collins Thesaurus   The entries in this thesaurus are arranged alphabetically so you can use it like a dictionary.

13 Book skills

' *Read the summary and the introduction first to see if the book's going to be useful.* '

' *Study a books' index, thinking of every possible description for the subject in question, as the index always seems to describe it under an unusual name.* '

Selecting and rejecting

Reading lists

You may be given long and daunting reading lists. Some lists will helpfully note which books are
  ** essential
  * recommended
    background reading, or reference only

If your list isn't divided up like this, and you feel rather overwhelmed, then ask your teacher or lecturer for advice.

In the library

The essential skill, once you have located the relevant section in the library, is to reject unhelpful books as speedily as possible, thus leaving more time for using your chosen books.

Purpose: If you are clear about *why* you are looking at these books then your searching is much more likely to be successful. Are you looking for

  a specific piece of information?
  a general summary or introduction to a subject?
  a chart or illustration?
  the explanation of a difficult term?
  a variety of viewpoints on a controversial subject?
  a thorough and scholarly treatment of a subject?
  references to further reading?

How to assess a book's usefulness – a checklist

Title	Remember that a short title can rarely indicate the scope of a book
Subtitle	This may indicate a level of difficulty, e.g. "a student's guide"
Author	How qualified and experienced is the author in this field? Look for information about the author on the title page, or on the front or back cover of the book. If the author has published any other works these may be listed on the back of the title page.
Publisher	A particular publisher may have a good reputation in a certain area, or simply be known as a reputable publisher.
Blurb	This is the information given on a book's back cover, or on the inside flap of a hardback's jacket. It is usually written by the publisher to sell the book, and often claims more for a book than an author would. Still it is a useful brief guide to what the book hopes to cover and achieve. It is sometimes more a statement of intent than of fact.
Date of publication	This appears on the reverse of the title page. The first date given, often after a © copyright sign, and the author's name, is the date of original publication, but remember the book will have been written at least twelve months before this date.

First published 1980
Fourth impression 1983

A new impression means the book has sold out, and been reprinted, usually with minor corrections.

First published 1979
Reprinted 1980, 1982
Second edition 1983

A new edition means that the author has thoroughly revised the text, and perhaps added new sections, while rewriting others, and bringing the whole work up-to-date.

Place of publication
This can be important in some subjects. If the book was published abroad the publisher's address will show this. If the book is simply an English translation, or an English edition of a book originally published overseas, then this will be stated:

First published in the United States 1975
First published in England 1982

Contents
This reveals at a glance the framework of the book.

List of illustrations/ diagrams
Older books often have a list of illustrations. A list of diagrams can indicate how comprehensive, and up-to-date, a book's coverage is. Turning first to a diagram or table may save you a considerable amount of reading.

Preface
This may state who the book is written for.

Introduction
This is written after the rest of the book, and often summarises the author's latest thinking about the subject.

Conclusion
If the book has a conclusion, reading it first can save you a lot of time. If you then decide to read the book through you will have a clear sense of the author's direction right from the beginning. Alternatively the opening or closing paragraphs of chapters may act as summaries.

Index
Some books have a separate name and subject index. Illustrations are referred to in **bold type,** and in many books major references to a topic, rather than just passing references, are noted in bold type.

Trade Councils 17, 43, **61-66**
Trade Unions 16, 19, 31, **48-60**
Unemployment 9, 12, 17, 33-36
Unions *see* Trade Unions
Wages 4, 18, 27, 38, 50-51

The term you are looking up may not be the term used in the index. Think of synonyms and other possible entries. If the book is American it is particularly likely that a different term will have been used.

Bibliography
(or References)
This is the list of sources which the writer has consulted. It will quickly indicate how broad and thorough the writer's research has been. By checking the dates of publication for the books listed in the bibliography you will be able to judge how up-to-date the author's work is.

● If you are going to make notes from a book note down the author, title, library code number, and page references. You never know when you may need to refer to the book again.

● If the book is a library book then do not mark it in any way, as this makes the book difficult to use for the next borrower.

Abbreviations used in footnotes in books

ibid. = in the same book as noted in the last footnote
op. cit. = in the book already mentioned
ff. = and the following pages

pp. = pages
cf. = compare
passim = to be found throughout a particular book

14 Reading

' *If I were starting again I'd do more background reading and not just the necessary work.* '

' *There are different techniques of reading for different types of books. If you're looking for a certain bit of information then don't read the whole page.* '

Reading for study

The largest part of a student's study time is spent reading. It is important that a student learns to

- manage the quantity of necessary reading effectively.
- read quickly with understanding.
- avoid irrelevant reading.
- identify different styles of reading which will be effective for various reading purposes.
- gain access to the most useful material available.
- read actively and resist episodes of passive reading which can arise.
- develop a questioning attitude to written material.

Throughout this chapter we will consider these points and return to them to analyse the effectiveness of your reading.

Now complete the first two columns of the table on the next page. Write in brief details of all the reading you have done in the last week or so. Consider all reading: chapters, texts, questions, essays, novels, lecture notes, articles, newspapers and computer printout.

Reading table

As you work through this chapter you will complete this table.

Reading matter	1 Time taken (mins)	2 Reading strategy Page 60	3 Skimming Page 62	4 Most effective strategy Page 67	5 Vocabulary Page 68	6 Usefulness Page 68	7 SQ3R Page 69

Reading strategies

A reader always has a purpose. The reading of a novel for enjoyment is somewhat different from the reading of the same novel for appreciation on an English literature course. In the same way, if you are looking for a piece of information then it is not necessary to read a book from page 1 to the end as you would read a novel.

This table describes six different reading strategies.

Reading strategy	Brief description	Purpose
Detailed reading	Means reading the whole passage carefully and thoughtfully trying to appreciate every point the author is making.	Complete understanding
Skimming	Means finding out what a chapter or a book is about.	General impression
Critical reading	Some authors write to persuade. You need to separate fact from opinion.	Making up your mind
Analytical reading	Means looking at the mechanics of the writing, studying the writer's skill.	Appreciate style and structure
Reading for enjoyment	Reading at whatever pace suits you. The more you read, the better reader you become.	Pleasure
Reading for information (scanning)	Looking for a specific detail by running your eye over the pages quickly.	Fact finding

Enter in the reading table (Column 2) which reading strategy you think you used in your recent reading.

p.59

Skimming

Every student would be more effective, and have more time, if skimming was part of their reading routine. Skimming can be used in two ways:

● in the selection and rejection of chapters or books for reading.
● as preparation before reading a chapter or book.

The volume of reading most students face is enormous: text books, set books, recommended book lists, periodicals, reports, and much special subject reading as well. Skimming allows you to sort the wheat from the chaff and creates the time for you to concentrate on important sections of reading matter. When you skim you do not read every word, instead you read:

● The title and subheadings
● The first sentence from each paragraph (or the first paragraph of a chapter)
● The last sentence of a passage (or the last paragraph of a chapter)
● A summary of the chapter first, if there is one

You should pay attention to any diagrams, charts or graphs.

Try skimming the following passage. Some questions are set at the end, read these first: these are your reading purpose. Before you start re-read the guide points.

Is the Ocean Bottom Moving?

The ocean bottom is very interesting to oceanographers from many points of view. For one thing they find that the sedimentary rocks that exist on the ocean bottom are much younger than any similar rocks they find on the continents. In fact, no deposits on the ocean floor seem to be older than a couple of hundred million years, whereas many rocks on the continents are far older than this. For many years geologists have been asking, "Why aren't there older rocks on the ocean bottom?" and "Where do the older rocks go?"

Furthermore, the mud layers covering the rocks on the bottom of the ocean – the sediments – are continually being deposited, and yet the thickness of this overall layer remains very thin. Again, scientists ask: "where do these sediments go?" "Why aren't the sediments much thicker on the ocean bottom than we find them to be?"

The answers to these questions have been found in modern measurements which indicate that the ocean bottom must be in motion. It is moving at a speed of from about one-half to six inches a year, and it seems to be doing so in a manner that suggests that the continents also are moving. Apparently the continents can be thought of as floating in a "sea" of basalt (that is, the ocean bottom rocks).

Scientists think that many millions of years ago all the continents were joined together in two huge land masses, called Laurasia and Gondwanaland. Later on in geological time, Laurasia split into North America, Europe, and Asia, while South America, Africa, Antarctica, and Australia were formed from Gondwanaland. But the final picture is apparently not complete, for the sea bottom is still moving and evidently the continents are moving too. Where they will be a few million years from now, scientists can only guess.

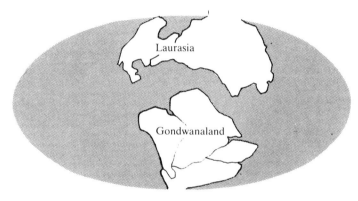

The two primeval continents, Laurasia, consisting of North America, Europe, and Asia; and Gondwanaland, consisting of South America, Africa, Antarctica, and Australia.

As far as oceanographers can now tell, the reason for this movement is that the rock beneath the earth's crust (the mantle) is a somewhat fluid substance. It will move in much the same manner as water, but of course much more slowly. With the earth being warmer in the interior, convective currents or vertical heat motions are set up in much the same way that air in a room moves from the floor to the ceiling when an electric heater is placed on the floor. Of course, when the moving mantle material reaches the underside of the crustal rocks (the ocean bottom), it spreads out to the sides. It is this horizontal motion that causes the ocean bottom and the continents to move.

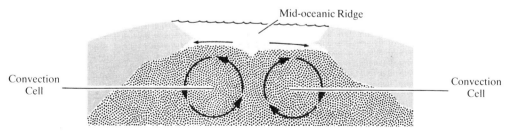

Convection cells in the earth's mantle causing motion of the ocean bottom.

Eventually, the mantle material must return to the interior of the earth, because any such material that comes from there must be replaced. In this manner, the older rocks on the underside of the oceanic crust are dragged down into the earth, which explains why the older rocks cannot be found. Similarly, the older sediments are also carried away as they build up. Measurements have been made that indicate that the rocks very close to the mid-Atlantic ridge in the North Atlantic Ocean have very recently risen from the interior of the earth, while at points farther away from the mid-Atlantic ridge, it was found that the age of the rocks increased. Thus, by noting the rock age measurements and the distance between samples, it is possible for scientists to calculate the rate at which the sea floor is spreading – which works out to be between one-half and six inches per year.

Extract from *Oceanography* Jerome Williams, Franklin Watts Ltd.

Questions

What is the passage about?

Does the passage explain why the ocean floor has few older rocks?

You can practise skimming while reading newspapers or magazines.

Skimming is a very useful preparation for reading a chapter or book in detail. This enables you to appreciate the structure of the topic and how parts of it inter-relate. As you skim your mental set is developing; your concentration will focus more strongly on your work rather than on any distractions.

Summaries

By reading the summary you will become aware of the destination of an argument or proof; this allows insight into the thinking which arises en route. Most of us read study books as we would read a thriller, the plot develops and comes to a conclusion. When reading study material it is essential that there is no mystery about what is to follow.

Indicate on the reading table (column 3) which parts of your reading were skimmed before you read them. Use a ●. Put a □ next to any part of your recent reading which would have been better skimmed, i.e. it would have helped your understanding and saved you time.  p.59

Reading table

As you work through this chapter you will complete this table.

Reading matter	1 Time taken (mins)	2 Reading strategy Page 60	3 Skimming Page 62	4 Most effective strategy Page 67	5 Vocabulary Page 68	6 Usefulness Page 68	7 SQ3R Page 69
Industry and Empire	All together 3 hours	mainly detailed	●		✓	A	SQ3R
Sunday Paper	½ hr	various	●	□		D	

Scanning

When you scan a page or a chapter you are looking for a piece of information. The brain can recognise what it is searching for extremely quickly, much faster than the time it takes to read the text.

Run your eye through this passage about Attingham Park, Shropshire. Who made the cast iron window frames which are part of the ceiling in the Attingham gallery?

Try scanning again to discover when the first Lord Berwick died. A pen might help to guide your eye when scanning. Obviously you don't continue to scan when you have located your information.

Tern Hall, a modest Queen Anne house built in 1701, was transformed some eighty years later into the classical mansion of Attingham Park by Noel Hill, 1st Baron Berwick, a great-nephew of the original builder.

Noel Hill inherited in 1783, and almost at once began to realize his ambitious plans to build a country seat on an extravagant and imposing scale. He changed the name of the house to Attingham, calling it after the medieval name of the parish of Atcham in which it stands, and he commissioned George Steuart as his architect. A Scotsman of considerable individuality of whose career little is known, Steuart was responsible for several houses and churches in Shropshire. A condition of his engagement was that the old Tern Hall should be incorporated in the new mansion. His solution was to build a central block, immediately in front of the existing structure, and to balance the unusual height and depth of the resultant building with twin flanking pavilions linked by colonnades. This huge façade is nearly 400 feet long and is given emphasis and cohesion by a central pedimented portico with four tall columns. Built of grey Grinshill ashlar and seen from the Tern bridge across the wide parkland that was land- scaped by Humphry Repton, Attingham's pale and stately shape dominates the gentle Shropshire landscape in almost alien fashion.

For all its size, Attingham does not contain a great deal of accommodation, nor a series of grandiose and brilliantly decorated apartments. Its internal arrangement is both unusual and unusually theoretical for an English country house. Two sets of rooms, one primarily masculine and the other feminine, lie on each side of the entrance hall. Lord Berwick's octagonal study and ante-room on the west side of the central block are balanced by Lady Berwick's drawing room and ante-room to the east.

Lord Berwick did not long enjoy his grand new mansion, for he died suddenly in 1789, leaving three sons who succeeded him in turn. The 2nd Lord Berwick travelled to Italy when he came of age in 1792. It was a momentous journey not only for him but for Attingham, as he spent lavishly on pictures and works of art. Ten years later, he commissioned Nash to make alterations to the house and to build a picture gallery. In the early 19th century, picture galleries in English houses were rarities – Stourhead has one – and those that existed were primarily for sculpture. Technically the Attingham gallery is interesting, for the ceiling is the earliest in which cast-iron window frames were used. They were made by the Coalbrookdale company a few miles away on the Severn. The result is an interesting exercise in Regency taste, with a hint of the later industrial influences so apparent in much mid-19th-century architecture. The collection housed in the gallery today was mostly acquired after the 1827 sale.

From *Attingham Park* National Trust Guide, Jonathan Cape.

Practice reading strategies

The exercise which follows is designed to give you practice in choosing and using the best reading style. The answers to the questions can be found in the passage opposite. Read each question carefully as it will become your purpose for reading and will help you to decide which of the six reading strategies (outlined on page 58) will be most appropriate. When you have chosen read the passage according to that style and then answer the question.

Question: What is a melt-down?

. . . .

. . . .

. . . .

. . . .

. . . .

Reading strategy used: →

Question: What was the original fault which resulted in the Three Mile Island accident?

. . . .

. . . .

. . . .

. . . .

. . . .

Reading strategy used: →

Question: Explain why the choice of fuel and high engineering standards, together with automatic shut-down procedures, are defences against a core melt-down?

. . . .

. . . .

. . . .

. . . .

. . . .

Reading strategy used: →

Defence in depth

The significance of melting

Like any large and complicated piece of engineering, a nuclear reactor can in principle go wrong in many different ways. Mostly these are minor malfunctions, easily overcome. A few are serious. Large operational safety manuals are written which analyse a multitude of conceivable faults in detail; and these have of course to be thoroughly understood and acted upon, by the operators, for the good running and general protection of the plant. There is a great economic incentive for this, quite apart from the need to protect the operators and the general public.

So far as public safety is concerned, what particularly distinguishes the serious from the minor accidents is the *melting* of the fuel, or the possibility of its melting. All those malfunctions which do not bring this about are of little more significance, in their effect on the public, than small everyday industrial accidents. The risk to the public becomes serious only when a large part of the fuel melts or becomes likely to do so. The reason is that most of the atoms responsible for the radioactive hazard in a reactor stay close to where they were created, inside the solid fuel or its enveloping can of cladding material. Once a radioactive atom has come to rest, after its creation, it is almost immobile inside a solid, being trapped in place by the densely packed and strongly bonded atoms of the material itself. But if the fuel melts, and if its can also fails – for example by bursting, melting or oxidising – then the mobility of the liquid gives the atoms plenty of freedom to move about. A large number, perhaps a tenth, of the volatile radioactive atoms could then escape into the coolant.

A natural defence against the large-scale release of radioactivity is therefore provided by the *solidity* and *continuity* of the fuel and of the metallic can in which it is sealed. So long as these remain intact, little radioactivity can escape. A good feature here is that the fuel used in most modern reactors consists of *uranium dioxide* (together with plutonium oxide in fast reactors) and this is an extremely stable and refractory substance with a melting point of about 2,800°C. Moreover, the melting points of the canning materials – zirconium alloy (about 1,800°C) and stainless steel (about 1,500°C) – are also fairly high. The Magnox reactors use materials which are less refractory – uranium metal (about 1,135°C) and magnesium alloy (about 650°C). But a compensating factor here is the low power density, only about 1 kilowatt per litre, which enables gas cooling even at atmospheric pressure to control temperatures due to decay heating.

Prevention of melt-downs

To avoid the possibility of a melt-down, the obvious first defence is to use extremely high standards of design, construction, inspection and operation, so that there is little chance of things going wrong. Naturally, all reactor specifications demand such standards. Although the quality of reactor engineering is very high, therefore, there is nonetheless always some possibility of human error creeping in. An absolutely immaculate standard in practice is unattainable. The occasional faulty item will slip through, or be put together badly, and not always be detected. An occasional mistake will sometimes be made in running the reactor – a wrongly closed valve, a false reading on an instrument, an ill-judged action. And so a further line of defence is necessary, in case an important fault develops despite the generally high engineering and operational standards. This further defence consists of various protective devices designed to take control of the faulty reactor and bring it to complete safety. An independent system of alternative power for circulating the coolant and activating the reactor controls is one obvious example. Others include the various independent emergency nuclear shut-down devices, and the emergency core cooling systems.

Defence in depth, therefore, results from the requirement that at least *two* independent major functions have to go wrong, at the same time, for a melt-down. As well as the original fault in the normal operating system, there has also to be a failure of an essential protective system for controlling this fault. Given the high standard of engineering, so that the probability of either going wrong is very small, and given a design and mode of operation which ensures that they are truly independent – in the sense that a fault in one cannot induce a fault in the other – then the chance of *both* going wrong at the same time is extremely small.

This is a good safety principle, but it has limitations. For example, although the two systems may be mechanically independent, they are nevertheless coupled together in the *mind* of the reactor operator. Through his attempts to manage the crisis, by taking charge of the controls manually, the fault in the normal system may influence the protective system. This happened at Three Mile Island. When the reactor suffered a loss-of-coolant fault as a result of a stuck valve, the operators were unfortunately led, from misleading instruments, to throttle down the emergency core cooling system, in the mistaken belief that the reactor was too full of water.

From *How safe is Nuclear Energy?* Alan Cotterell F.R.S., Heinemann.

Use the passage opposite to answer these questions.

Question: If you were in Jim's place would the shorthand writer in the courtroom have such a strong effect on you?

. . . .

. . . .

Reading strategy used: →

Question:
i   To what extent has the writer adopted the style of his character, Jim, in this extract?
ii How effectively is the flashback technique used here?

i . . . .

. . . .

. . . .

ii . . . .

. . . .

Reading strategy used: →

Question: Is this a fair description of the way police behave during marches and in court?

. . . .

. . . .

. . . .

. . . .

. . . .

Reading strategy used: →

From The common good

Jim got a real shock of surprise when Sergeant Webster took the stand. For a start he wasn't in uniform. He was about forty, and very smartly dressed in a neat grey suit and a snowy white shirt. He had dark curly hair and a sort of friendly, pleasant face. For a moment Jim couldn't believe it was the same bloke. He had a sudden, crazy, notion that they'd put someone else in the witness box, someone pretending to be the sergeant. But that was daft. Even his voice was different, though; soft, and calm, and reasonable.

'I swear by Almighty God that the evidence that I give shall be the truth, the whole truth and nothing but the truth.'

It was absurd. Jim shivered. He remembered the sergeant's snarling, contorted face as he'd grabbed his arm and twisted it up his back until he'd screamed. He remembered the way, later, in the police station, he'd punched him in the stomach, and kicked him, and spat in his face. It was unbelievable.

The Sergeant's evidence was brief, and to the point, and sounded utterly reasonable. On the day of the march, he said, he had been in command of a group of thirty constables out of the total force of several hundreds. The area in which he had been controlling the crowds had been a particularly violent one, and several policemen had been injured, some of them seriously. The crowd, which had consisted mostly of Asians, with pockets of politically motivated whites, had been abusive and highly provocative. At first insults, then stones, sticks and bottles had been thrown. He had led several charges into the crowd, and made several arrests. On one of the charges he had seen the defendant, James Arthur Barker, holding a half-wallbrick which he clearly intended to throw at the police. His right arm was drawn back, his body was in a throwing stance, and he was shouting obscenities at the advancing officers. Yes, he could identify James Arthur Barker as the youth in the court; there. He was arrested and taken to Albert Road police station where he was formally cautioned, and charged with threatening behaviour and carrying an offensive weapon. At the police station he had been abusive, violent and had attempted to punch two police officers and kick another in the groin. A certain amount of force had had to be applied to bring him under control.

The sergeant looked round the court with a pleasant, honest look when he'd said his piece. Jim looked at his solicitor, Mr Ellerman, half expecting him to jump up and tear the story to pieces. Then he remembered. Mr Ellerman had said he wasn't going to cross-examine unless something was said that they weren't going to break down in their own evidence. He knew what he was doing, Jim was sure of that. He tried to relax, but he was shaken. It was incredible. It was a pack of lies, it was awful. Mr Ellerman indicated that he had no questions and the sergeant smiled and stepped down. As Jim looked up, so did the shorthand girl, and their eyes met. He felt a deep blush rise in his cheeks. He felt ashamed. What must she be thinking of him? It was awful.

From *A sense of shame and other stories* Jan Needle, Andre Deutsch.

Return to the reading table and write in column 4 the reading strategy which would have been most effective for each piece of your reading.

p.59

Reading speed

> *I took a speed reading course, learning to read straight*
> *down the middle of the page, and I was able to go through*
> *War and Peace in 20 minutes. It's about Russia.*
> Woody Allen

It is a tempting thought that we might double our rate of learning if we could read twice as fast. A student reads to learn and learning is a process which takes time. If we read faster than we can learn, confusion, misconceptions and poor recall are likely to result.

It is useful to consider reading and learning as one. When the information is easy to understand, because it is familiar or is closely linked to existing knowledge, then it is more efficient to increase the speed of reading. Harder material demands a slower reading rate; perhaps reading it twice is likely to yield a better understanding. In other words good students will vary their reading speed to suit the reading matter.

Research suggests that students slow down when they read difficult material but that they are unlikely to speed up when straightforward text and ideas are studied.

A flexible approach to reading speed will develop only with practice. The first stage is to identify the appropriate reading strategy. Detailed reading will often be required but it should not be the automatic choice. Newspapers contain such a variety of articles that you can practise all of the different reading strategies. Having identified the appropriate strategy try to consciously control the rate at which you read. Notice the difference in the speed at which you read.

Using a newspaper:
- **Skim** the first few pages to find which story you most want to read.
- **Read** the story *carefully*, be aware of your reading rate.
- **Scan** the classified advertisements for a particular object you might like to buy.
- **Read** the newspapers *opinion* column (the editorial). Separate fact from opinion.

Reasons for poor reading

1 Failure to recognise your reading purpose. Without a clear idea of why you are reading you are unlikely to be effective.

2 Failure to vary the pace of reading: this results in too slow or too fast processing of the information in the brain. During the slow phase the reader is more easily distracted, during the fast phase the reader will become confused.

3 Slow readers will lose the sense of what they are reading more easily. They will recognise this has happened and back-track. This takes time and further delays the appreciation of the piece.

4 Readers who do not recognise the 'markers' in the text (headings, paragraphs, introduction, conclusion, graphs and charts, order in arguments), will find it difficult to make good sense of the passage.

5 Pronouncing the words as you read slows down reading. This habit, often stemming from the time when we were first taught to read, must be broken. The best way to do this is to read more quickly so that vocalisation is impossible; light reading matter should be used for these exercises.

6 Failure to make notes, underline key words or use other forms of active reading always reduces effectiveness.

7 A limited vocabulary is a serious hindrance to effective and efficient reading and understanding. (See *Widening your vocabulary* page 88)

Put a ✓ in column 5 of the reading table if the reading matter had no words which you needed to check for meaning. ⟵ p.59

Reading to learn and remember: SQ3R

Rate how useful the material in the reading table is from the viewpoint of your studies. Use a scale A (very useful) to E (useless), enter the numbers in column 6. ⟵ p.59

SQ3R is a very well known method of reading and rembering. Good students, about to employ SQ3R, will have a clear idea of what they need to learn. Their first task is to Ⓢkim the book or chapter to make sure it is relevant to their study. By skimming the student will also prepare mental set and he or she will be less likely to be distracted.

Ⓢkim
Ⓠuestion
Ⓡead
Ⓡeview
Ⓡemember

Of course skimming is a useful way of getting into your stride. You should frame your study purpose as a (Q)uestion or questions. Bear these in mind as you read, because they are your reading purpose and they ensure active reading. It is very easy to read mechanically without thinking about the reading matter.

You must be alert, active and enquiring as you read.

The next stage is to (R)ead the book or chapter carefully, paying attention to graphs, diagrams and charts. If it is your own book consider using a yellow highlighter pen to draw your attention to important points. Clarify any points and check the meaning of any words you don't understand, as soon as you can.

Now you must (R)eview the material. Have you answered the questions you set yourself? If not you need to reread the relevant section. The period of review allows your brain time to order the new information (see page 31). If the work is important it should be reviewed again after a day and then after a week and so on. After carrying out the first four stages you should (R)emember the work better.

Practise SQ3R on the following passage. Before you start, read the question which will be your purpose for reading.

Question: What evidence is there to suggest the men behind the Industrial Revolution were scientists and men of conscience rather than hard-headed businessmen?

After each stage of SQ3R complete this checklist below.

Skim:	What is it about?	☐
	Is it likely to answer the question?	☐
	Do you appreciate the structure of the passage?	☐
Question:	Are you clear about what information you are seeking in the text?	☐
	How should this information be organised?	☐
	Have any more questions arisen during the reading of the passage?	☐
Read:	Are there any words you need to look up?	☐
	What are the key words?	☐
Review	Answer the questions, review the passage again if you need to?	☐
Remember:	What revision method would you use to remember this material?	☐

Complete the reading table by writing SQ3R in column 7 for any part of your study reading which might be better done using this method. ◁ p.59

From The drive for power

The men who made the Industrial Revolution are usually pictured as hardfaced businessmen with no other motive than self-interest. That is certainly wrong. For one thing, many of them were inventors who had come into business that way. And for another, a majority of them were not members of the Church of England but belonged to a puritan tradition in the Unitarian and similar movements. John Wilkinson was much under the influence of his brother-in-law Joseph Priestley, later famous as a chemist, but who was a Unitarian minister and was probably the pioneer of the principle, 'the greatest happiness of the greatest number'.

Joseph Priestley, in turn, was scientific adviser to Josiah Wedgwood. Now Wedgwood we usually think of as a man who made marvellous tableware for aristocracy and royalty: and so he did, on rare occasions, when he got the commission. For example, in 1774 he made a service of nearly a thousand highly decorated pieces for Catherine the Great of Russia, which cost over £2000 – a great deal of money in the coin of that day. But the base of that tableware was his own pottery, creamware; and in fact all the thousand pieces, undecorated, cost less than £50, yet looked and handled like Catherine the Great's in every way except for the hand-painted idylls. The creamware which made Wedgwood famous and prosperous was not porcelain, but a white earthenware pottery for common use. That is what the man in the street could buy, at about a shilling a piece. And in time that is what transformed the kitchens of the working class in the Industrial Revolution.

Wedgwood was an extraordinary man: inventive, of course, in his own trade, and also in the scientific techniques that might make his trade more exact. He invented a way of measuring the high temperatures in the kiln by means of a sort of sliding scale of expansion in which a clay test-piece moved. Measuring high temperatures is an ancient and difficult problem in the manufacture of ceramics and metals, and it is fitting (as things went then) that Wedgwood was elected to the Royal Society.

Josiah Wedgwood was no exception; there were dozens of men like him. Indeed, he belonged to a group of about a dozen men, the Lunar Society of Birmingham (Birmingham was then still a scattered group of industrial villages), who gave themselves the name because they met near the full moon. This was so that people like Wedgwood, who came from a distance to Birmingham, should be able to travel safely over wretched roads that were dangerous on dark nights.

But Wedgwood was not the most important industrialist there: that was Matthew Boulton, who brought James Watt to Birmingham because there they could build the steam engine. Boulton was fond of talking about measurement; he said that nature had destined him to be an engineer by having him born in the year 1728, because that is the number of cubic inches in a cubic foot. Medicine was important in that group also, for there were new and important advances being made. Dr William Withering discovered the use of digitalis in Birmingham. One of the doctors who has remained famous, who belonged to the Lunar Society, was Erasmus Darwin, the grandfather of Charles Darwin. The other grandfather? Josiah Wedgwood.

Societies like the Lunar Society represent the sense of the makers of the Industrial Revolution (that very English sense) that they had a social responsibility. I call it an English sense, though in fact that is not quite fair; the Lunar Society was much influenced by Benjamin Franklin and by other Americans associated with it. What ran through it was a simple faith: the good life is *more* than material decency, but the good life must be based on material decency.

It took a hundred years before the ideals of the Lunar Society became reality in Victorian England. When it did come, the reality seemed commonplace, even comic, like a Victorian picture postcard. It is comic to think that cotton underwear and soap could work a transformation in the lives of the poor. Yet these simple things – coal in an iron range, glass in the windows, a choice of food – were a wonderful rise in the standard of life and health. By our standards, the industrial towns were slums, but to the people who had come from a cottage, a house in a terrace was a liberation from hunger, from dirt, and from disease; it offered a new wealth of choice. The bedroom with the text on the wall seems funny and pathetic to us, but for the working class wife it was the first experience of private decency. Probably the iron bedstead saved more women from childbed fever than the doctor's black bag, which was itself a medical innovation.

These benefits came from mass production in factories. And the factory system was ghastly; the schoolbooks are right about that. But it was ghastly in the old traditional way. Mines and workshops had been dank, crowded and tyrannical long before the Industrial Revolution. The factories simply carried on as village industry had always done, with a heartless contempt for those who worked in them.

From *The Ascent of Man*, Jacob Bronowski, BBC and Angus and Robertson.

FACT SHEET

The best conditions for reading

It is easy to underestimate the importance of the correct level of lighting and comfort for a reader. Highly motivated readers will read standing on a train, in front of a television set or in a busy canteen or refectory. Nevertheless when the motivation is lower, reading conditions become more important.

Make sure the text is evenly lit. A very bright light can produce too sharp a contrast between print and the background. Eye fatigue can cause headaches which can cut short study sessions. Some study lamps with 60 or 100 watt bulbs can create this effect. Use a low power lamp, or diffuse or reflect the light from a high power lamp.
Trying to read in poor light also strains the eyes. Poor lighting is quickly identified but sometimes, when a study session continues into the evening, the lighting conditions deteriorate slowly enough to deceive.

low power direct lighting

high power reflected lighting

A good posture when reading is important for two reasons. Firstly so much time is spent reading that the effect of poor posture can remain with us days, weeks or even years later. Secondly you should try to keep your back straight, sit in an upright chair with your back against the back of the chair. The reading material should be at a height which makes it possible for you to keep your neck and shoulders from bending forward too much. Desks and study surfaces are constructed with this in mind and if it proves difficult for you to read in this way your eyesight might need attention.

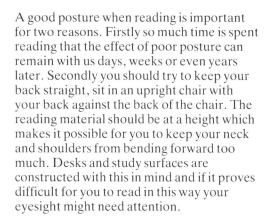

It is helpful to vary your reading position and location from time to time. This movement is healthy and can improve your concentration.

15 Essay writing

> *At college there are more essays, they involve more thought and you can't just rely on the teacher's notes.*

What sort of essays will you be asked to write?

Below sixth form level the majority of essays you had to write told a story in one way or another.

Creative writing asks for an imaginative response usually written in a story form.

Factual essays ask you to "describe", "give an account of" or "narrate" (tell the story of) something. Facts are usually more important than opinions in this type of essay, and you rarely have the chance to give your own viewpoint or interpretation. Instead you need to show that you know the answers to questions about your subject such as

What happened?
How did it happen?
When?
Where?

In scientific essays you have to explain, for example, a theory, process or phenomena.

At sixth form level and beyond the great majority of essays are analytical. **The analytical essay** requires you to interpret and comment on one aspect of a subject, for example

- Discuss the effects of public health reform on social conditions in Victorian England.
- How significant a role does fate play in the novels of Thomas Hardy?
- Was the dissolution of the monasteries primarily a religious, economic or political phenomenon?

Read the following list of essay titles, and by paying close attention to the question words in the title, note beside each whether a factual or analytical essay is required:
- "The British press, while claiming to be politically independent, is controlled by a handful of owners with a vested interest in the status quo". Do you agree?
- Give an account of the events which led up to the outbreak of the First World War.
- Should we play games with South Africa?
- Describe the character of Piggy in *Lord of the Flies*. Illustrate your answer by close reference to episodes in the novel.
- Account for the American withdrawal from the Vietnam War.

There are 6 key stages in writing an analytical essay:

1 Choosing a title
2 Researching for relevant information
3 Planning
4 Writing
5 Presenting the essay, including the use of quotes, sources and footnotes
6 Checking

Stage 1 Choosing a title

Select the title which gives you the best opportunity to write a coherent and relevant essay. If possible choose a title which interests you, or on which you have already done some work. If you don't fully understand a title, or find it difficult to relate to your understanding of the subject, then either choose a simpler title or seek advice. Just because a title is long does not necessarily make it more difficult to write about. Consider these titles:

a Assess the importance of trade unionism in this century.
b Consider the impact which the growth of mass trade unions have had on the relationship between employee and employed. How successfully have employers attempted to cope with this challenge to their traditional authority?

What would you say was the chief difference between the 2 titles?

. . . .

. . . .

. . . .

For our view of the difference see under Stage 3 Planning, page 77.

Stage 2 Researching

 Collect all the information first. If the essay is in parts underline the information you are going to use for the various sections in different coloured pens.

Unless you are going to be content with regurgitating notes you have already been given, you will need to undertake some research for your essay. At its simplest level research might just involve you in following up a few references to books or articles which you have been told to consult. Even here, however, there may be difficulties caused by a shortage of the recommended books, so you may have to discover other sources for yourself.

However limited your research you will be able to save yourself a considerable amount of time if you know how to make the best use of a library and its contents: See *Library and research skills*, page 48 and *Book skills*, page 56.

Before you begin researching make sure you know what sort of an essay the title demands:

analysis
description
explanation
detailed commentary
comparison
evaluation

The recommended length of the essay (usually from 500 to 2500 words) will indicate how much depth and detail will be expected. If your handwriting is of average size you will get about eight words to a line, and approximately 250 words to each side of A4 paper.

Having studied the question ask yourself "What exactly do I need to find out?". Your research must be selective and clearly directed at the essay title. (See SQ3R, page 68)

Stage 3 Planning

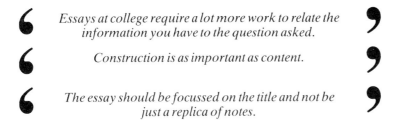

Essays at college require a lot more work to relate the information you have to the question asked.

Construction is as important as content.

The essay should be focussed on the title and not be just a replica of notes.

This is the vital stage at which you relate and link your ideas, together with what you have discovered during your research, to the title. Planning helps to clarify your thoughts.

Why plan? Planning an essay is as important as drawing up plans for a building. It ensures that your finished product has firm foundations, meets your requirements, and will stand up to critical scrutiny.

Planning
- Ensures that you stick to the point
- Organises the essay in a coherent way
- Makes you think about priorities
- Saves time
- Prevents the essay from being a series of unconnected paragraphs
- Gives the reader a clear sense of direction. This makes the essay much easier to read

Remember: The person who marks your essay will not wish to read all you know about a subject; instead she or he will want to see that you have been able to understand the title, and to relate your knowledge to the question being asked.

Ways of planning

Compare these 3 different methods of planning for the following essay title:

"Public transport is more socially equitable, and makes more efficient use of scarce resources." Comment on this view by referring to several methods of transport.

Method 1

Public transport may be more equitable in theory, but in practice it is not as efficient as private enterprise at the speedy movement of people. Cars move people quickly to where they want to go whereas public transport can be slow though this doesn't apply to inter-city trains. Public transport does let some people, eg OAPs, travel cheaply but particularly in the countryside buses and trains are slow and infrequent. If you need to travel a long way then flying is fastest. Concorde does use a lot of fuel, and has been a great burden on the taxpayer however it has enabled VIPs to get about very quickly which helps ordinary people in the long run.

Method 2

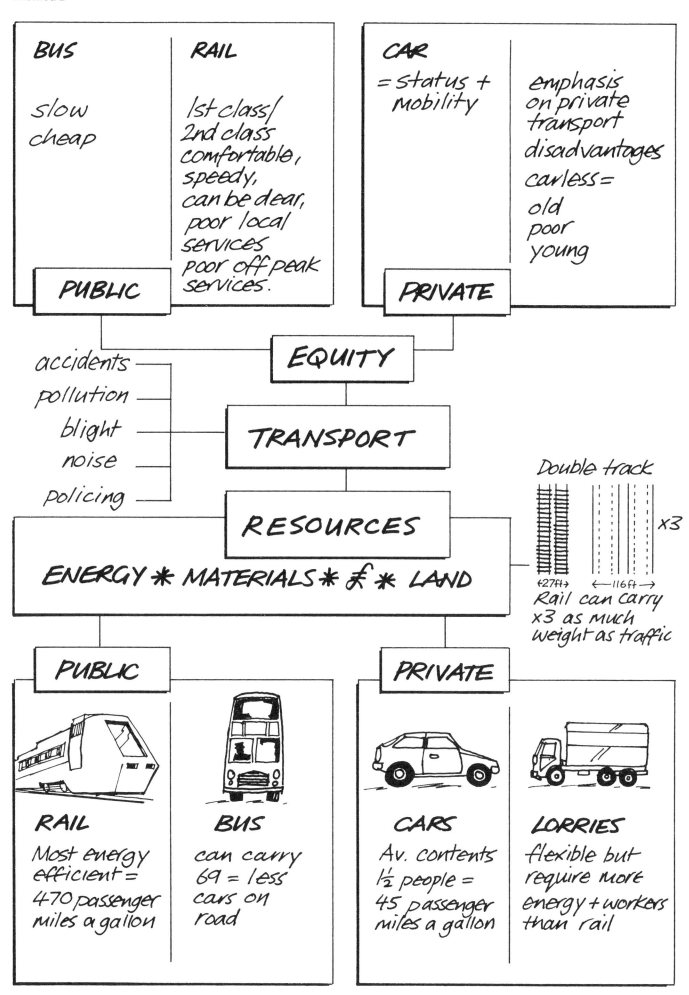

BUS

slow
cheap

RAIL

1st class/
2nd class
comfortable,
speedy,
can be dear,
poor local
services
poor off peak
services.

PUBLIC

CAR
= status +
mobility

emphasis
on private
transport
disadvantages
carless =
old
poor
young

PRIVATE

EQUITY

accidents
pollution
blight
noise
policing

TRANSPORT

RESOURCES

ENERGY * MATERIALS * £ * LAND

Double track

←27ft→   ←116ft→   x3

Rail can carry
x3 as much
weight as traffic

PUBLIC

RAIL

Most energy
efficient =
470 passenger
miles a gallon

BUS

can carry
69 = less
cars on
road

PRIVATE

CARS

Av. contents
1½ people =
45 passenger
miles a gallon

LORRIES

flexible but
require more
energy + workers
than rail

Method 3

EQUITABLE?

PUBLIC TRANSPORT

Open to all	Rail quite dear
Concessions to O.A.P's, students	Transport only to places on route. Lack of Govt investment = poor service. Routes closed. Esp in country areas.

PRIVATE TRANSPORT

Confers mobility and flexibility	42% households no car.
Easier on old and disabled (door to door)	Mobility according to income not need. Tax subsidies to manufacturers business users, lorries.

RESOURCES

PUBLIC TRANSPORT

Investment in rail just over $\frac{1}{3}$ that needed for M/way	Capital costs seem higher ... no hidden subsidies (eg. policing, lighting)
More energy efficient than private transport.	

PRIVATE TRANSPORT

Supports motor manufacturers	Pollution/lead poisoning). Accidents (cost to Health service) Noise Vibration Stress (pedestrians + cyclists) Prime land for car parks

!! WORTH MENTIONING !!

AIR: Greater speed = more energy, eg Concorde. (Massive public subsidy)

"Tell me how fast you can go and I'll tell you who you are"
                                                    "Ivan Illich"

Now plan an essay on the title "When unemployment rises social unrest is bound to become more prevalent". Discuss.

Some essay titles provide you with a skeleton of a plan because they break down the topic into its chief elements. For example, title **B** in Stage 1 of this chapter (page 73):

Consider the impact which the growth of mass trade unions have had on the relationship between employee and employed. How successfully have employers attempted to cope with this challenge to their traditional authority?

This title immediately divides itself up into sections:

1 Trade union impact on worker and boss relationship
2 Employers' measures to combat union power. Success?

Stage 4 Writing

> *Get down to the point and don't waffle.*

> *It's probably better to prepare and think about essays during the week, then write them up at the weekend. But it's most important to put a time limit on the writing.*

> *Science essays require little style but they do require ordered sequence – introduction, a number of points covered in single paragraphs, and a conclusion.*

> *Don't take hours over them. In the exam you only have 45 minutes.*

> *Use diagrams where possible to make the essay more interesting.*

> *Think them out first. Make a rough copy and then check it before writing it up. Make sure you've included all the points asked for in the title. I leave essays to the weekend so I can spend a whole day on one thing.*

Your essay needs to be sufficiently well written so that

1 Your meaning is clear to the reader
2 It shows you have understood the title
3 It shows a coherent line of thought
4 It demonstrates that you can distinguish between the relevant and the irrelevant

Compare the following opening paragraphs on the topic

● What do you understand by the term "civilization"? Do you consider that some ways of life are more civilized than others?

A

Although modern man sets himself apart from other animals by saying that he alone can make fire, this is becoming less true. While almost every person can operate a lighter, or strike a match, how many members of the technical, Western World could, when given two pieces of wood and some natural fuel, build a cooking flame? Not many. Yet, to the "savage," "backward" tribes of primitive society, this is still a common skill.

B CIVILIZATION! It's strange to think you have just read a twelve letter word which was used as a pretence to exploit the Third World. It is a word which dictionaries strive to define, a word which professors profess about, a word which is supposed to put us above Stone Age Man and finally a word about which essays are written.

C In this essay I intend to explain the differences, as I see them, between the people in the western and third worlds. Civilization, as we know it, depends on all the aids of a modern technological society: machines, electricity, computers and above all silicon chips. I will demonstrate in this essay however, that this is far from being the case in the underdeveloped world. I will consider whether this means that people outside Europe and the USA are therefore less civilized. Here is a simple example to illustrate my point: in England we often see the ugly remains of a fire somewhere in the countryside, or perhaps near a campsite, but less developed peoples like the Aboriginals, take great care to spread out their ashes and to hide the remains of their fires. On the other hand, how well would tribesmen cope if they came to live in one of our big cities? Would they even be able to open a tin of beans? I doubt it.

D *Contrary to popular belief, being civilized DOES NOT depend on being technologically advanced, that is to say you do not need a television set, a motor car and other such silicon chip controlled luxuries. In fact you could even go so far as to say that, possibly, tribesmen and women are better off living in ignorance of these and other such things.*

E We are the so called civilised part of the world. We have television, space invaders, rockets to send men to the moon, and bombs that kill people but leave buildings intact. We wear expensive clothes and make-up to make us look beautiful so that we can be accepted. in society. These expensive clothes are often made of animal skins and furs, and the make-up is often made of, and tested on, animals. Money is everything, and without it you can't get by. The rich get richer and the poor get poorer. Civilization has gone too far.

F There are many different cultures in the world but many people in the western hemisphere have only one conception of "civilization", that being a highly educated society, well advanced in social development with a high level of equity. 'Primitive' people certainly lead a different way of life from ours, but does that imply that they are uncivilized?

Which of these extracts is apparently not on the point?

. . . .

Which seems to address the title in the most structured way?

. . . .

Which seems to address the title in the most interesting way?

. . . .

Which shows the most potential, and makes you want to read on?

. . . .

Complete the table below with a brief comment about each extract

	Relevance	Structure	Clarity	Interest	Examples
A					
B					
C					
D					
E					
F					

Style

A plain and concisely written essay allows your reader to focus clearly on what you are saying. Flowery writing, and the use of clichés and jargon, distract attention from what you are saying, and instead call attention to the way you are saying it. For this reason advertisers, politicians and journalists often use these devices.

Flowery writing is writing that is too ornate and fussy for an essay, for example
> *If I may be allowed to proffer an alternative opinion, albeit a personal one . . .*

Clichés are phrases that are so over used that they have lost their original meaning and sharpness, and have now become a substitute for thought. (A cliché is literally a printers' term for words and phrases so often used that they were kept set in a block of metal type, instead of being made up each time from individual letters). Example:
> *He made sure no stone was left unturned . . .*

Jargon (called "Gobbledygook" in America) is technical or specialised vocabulary which is often used unnecessarily, particularly to confuse, mislead or impress ordinary people. Examples: *Extravehicular Mobility Unit* (a space suit); *Surreptitious Entry* (burglary); *Material Operating Defect* (a mistake).

Slang is essentially oral and colloquial, and is therefore inappropriate for essays. Slang often originates as an escape from the plainness or occasional triteness of formal English. Slang can quickly become hackneyed through indiscriminate over-use; meaning and sharpness blur as the same words are regurgitated to save the effort of seeking more precise ones. Examples: *She kept going on about . . . He was dead lucky.*

Notice the flaws in style in the following passage:

> *At this moment in time the necessity of maintaining and supplementing incrementally a nuclear deterrent is obvious to the man in the street. If we were to become embroiled in a confrontation situation with a potentially hostile nation state we would wish to have the capacity to pacify the situation by being able to deploy, at a moment's notice, a nuclear 'shot across the bows'. In this day and age gunboat diplomacy is obsolescent, and we should feel naked without the presence of our nuclear shield.*

Avoid using "etc." in your essays; it is vague and suggests you are not quite sure of what you are writing about.

FACT SHEET

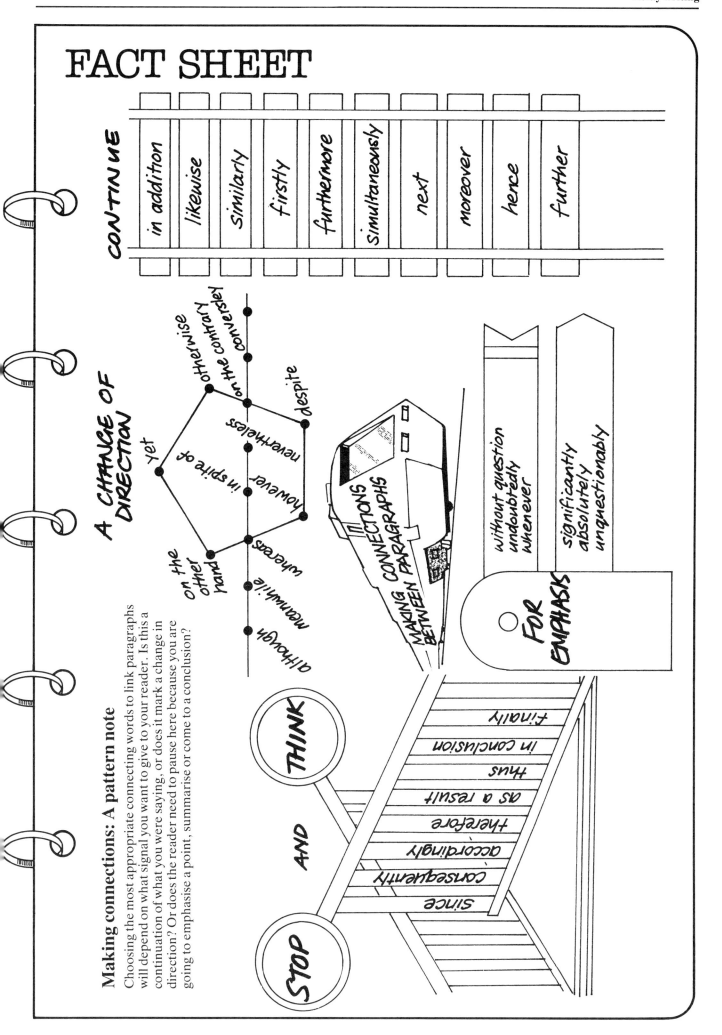

CONTINUE

in addition
likewise
similarly
firstly
furthermore
simultaneously
next
moreover
hence
further

A CHANGE OF DIRECTION

otherwise
on the contrary
yet
despite
nevertheless
in spite of
however
on the other hand
whereas
meanwhile
although

MAKING CONNECTIONS BETWEEN PARAGRAPHS

FOR EMPHASIS

without question
undoubtedly
whenever

significantly
absolutely
unquestionably

STOP

AND

THINK

since
consequently
accordingly
therefore
as a result
thus
in conclusion
finally

Making connections: A pattern note

Choosing the most appropriate connecting words to link paragraphs will depend on what signal you want to give to your reader. Is this a continuation of what you were saying, or does it mark a change in direction? Or does the reader need to pause here because you are going to emphasise a point, summarise or come to a conclusion?

Stage 5 Presentation
The use of primary and secondary sources

It is important to tell your reader what evidence, or sources, you are basing your arguments on, for example, an art student will refer to particular paintings while a historian will quote from historical documents. There are two types of source material: primary sources and secondary sources.

Primary sources (or evidence) are the raw materials of the essay. They are the originals. Primary sources are a part of the subject of the essay itself. Examples of primary sources would be:

- an extract from *Pride and Prejudice* for an essay about Jane Austen
- an extract from Domesday Book for an essay about Norman England
- census figures for an essay on population
- a painting by Picasso for an essay on modern art
- experimental results for a scientific report

Secondary sources are the interpretations, commentaries, essays and books written about the primary sources. Each new generation of scholars and writers interprets the primary sources in a slightly different way. Examples of secondary sources would be:

- a critical commentary on Jane Austen's novels
- a historian's view of the Norman Conquest
- a demographer's analysis of population trends
- an art critic's interpretation of Picasso's work
- an article in *New Scientist* about some recent experimental results

Read the following extracts and note beside each whether they are a primary or secondary source:

> Amateur was just what Turner was not as an artist. He trained the hard, the thorough way, not just in the Royal Academy Schools but as a topographical draughtsman for the engraver and as a copyist of other men's works. This last task, the copying of drawings by J R Cozens and other artists for Dr Monro over a period of three years, was all-important to him in getting to know the alternative tradition: the imaginative use of landscape instead of the 'tame delineation' of an object beautiful, interesting or picturesque in itself.
>
> Martin Butlin in *Turner 1775-1851*, 1974, p. 9,
> with permission from the Tate Gallery Publications Department

Table 6.15 Availability of durable goods: by household type, 1970 and 1979

		United Kingdom					*Percentages*	
	Pensioner households		Other households without children		Other households with children		All households	
	1970	1979	1970	1979	1970	1979	1970	1979
Percentage of households with:								
Telephone	25	53	38	70	37	73	35	67
Washing machine	41	57	61	73	81	92	65	77
Refrigerator	45	81	69	93	73	97	66	92
Deep-freezer	..	26	..	48	..	59	..	47
Car	17	26	57	65	63	72	52	58
Central heating	21	44	27	54	36	63	30	55
Television								
Colour	1	47	2	66	1	78	2	66
Black and white only	81	48	88	28	95	20	90	30

Central Statistical Office, *Social Trends 1982*, p. 111,
with permission from the Controller of Her Majesty's Stationery Office

Tragedy is not easily defined and the simple notion that it involves a 'fall' from a high position to a lower one will not suffice for most of the English tragic plays of this period. A different conception of 'falling' may be more revealing, however, especially if it can be allowed that the idea of a greater and farther-reaching 'Fall' lies behind such a notion for a society whose values and metaphors spring from those of Christianity. The concept of falling from a 'good' position to a 'bad' one may then be said to have as a corollary that of falling from a state of unity to one of dis-unity, since unity in Christian terms pre-supposes unity with God and the state is one of grace, whereas dis-unity involves the idea of separation from God in a state of disgrace.

Terence Hawkes, *Shakespeare and the Reason* 1964, pp. 35-6,
Routledge and Kegan Paul Ltd.

Women are told from their infancy and taught by the example of their mothers, that a little knowledge of human weakness, justly termed cunning, softness of temper, 'outward' obedience and a scrupulous attention to a puerile kind of propriety, will obtain for them the protection of man.

Mary Wollstonecraft, *The Vindication of the Rights of Women*, 1792, p. 33

One evening of late summer, before the nineteenth century had reached one-third of its span, a young man and woman, the latter carrying a child, were approaching the large village of Weydon-Priors, in Upper Wessex, on foot. They were plainly but not ill clad, though the thick hoar of dust which had accumulated on their shoes and garments from an obviously long journey lent a disadvantageous shabbiness to their appearance just now.

Thomas Hardy, *The Mayor of Casterbridge* 1886, p. 1

A personal experience, or one of your family's, may *seem* to have a connection with an essay title, but only *rarely* will the experience be both relevant and appropriate to include. In the following example, however, a student has made good use of personal experience as an introduction to some more general points on prejudice.

My father recalls his boyhood in the East End of London, where different types of cultures lived together. It was a poor, immigrant area, near the docks. Immigrants came over to seek a better life and they brought with them foreign habits, clothes and language. There was obvious resentment from the local people: local youths would attack the children of immigrant families, who in turn formed gangs to protect themselves.

This resentment expressed itself in a larger way in the rise of the fascist movement, which exploited cultural differences for political purposes.

The use of quotations

It is best to keep quotations, from both primary and secondary sources, short in your essays. The person who is going to read and mark your essay will know both the primary and secondary sources and will be interested in the comments you make about the quotations, and in how well you have related your quotes to your arguments. In a good essay the quotes form an integral part of the argument. In a poor essay the quotes stand out as ill-digested raw materials.

Short quotes, of up to a line in length, should simply be put in quotation marks. Longer quotes should begin on a new line about 4cm in from the margin. If you are typing you should double space the essay, but just use single spacing for longer quotes.

Summary: Choose appropriate, brief quotes, and explain clearly how they are relevant to the point you are making.

Bibliography and references

As well as using quotes in your essay you should name the sources you have read, or referred to, in the bibliography (list of books) at the end of your essay.

The advantages of a bibliography are:

● You can return to any of the sources at a later date because you have the exact reference at hand.
● Your reader can see how widely you have read.
● Your reader can check your evidence or sources.

Note
1 The library code (classification) number from the spine of the book.
2 Author's name, with the surname first in block capitals, followed by the author's first name(s).
3 Title
4 Year of first publication (found on the back of the title page).

Example:

330 TAWNEY, Richard Henry, Religion and the rise of capitalism, 1926

Footnotes For University level essays only.
Footnotes are used in more detailed and scholarly essays for two purposes:

1 To give a reference to a book quoted, or referred to, in your essay:
C Platt, *Medieval England*, p 249

2 To give interesting or additional details which are not sufficiently important or relevant to go into the main body of the essay.

Footnotes should be numbered and can either appear at the bottom of each page in the essay, which is easiest for the reader, or in a list at the end, which is more convenient if you are typing.

Appearance of the finished essay

If an essay looks well presented, in other words it is neat, clearly written and well paragraphed, then whoever is reading or marking it starts off with a favourable impression.

Typing

This gives a more professional appearance to your work, making it easier to read, and revise from. You should use double spacing, and type on one side of the page only. This will allow space for additions later on. A margin of about 4cm allows the person marking your essay to make marginal comments.

Keep a copy

If an essay has taken some time to write then it is worth keeping a copy just in case the original gets lost. You could either make a carbon copy or photocopy the essay. As a second best you could keep your rough draft or plan.

Word processing

See page 101.

RECORD SHEET

Checklist for essay writing

Read through this Checklist when you have chosen your title. Write the title on the right. Check off the points at each stage.

Essay titles

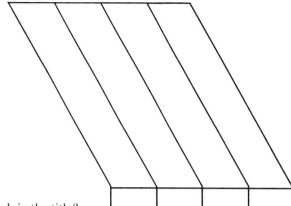

Stage 1:
Choosing a title

Have I identified the key words in the title?

Stage 2:
Researching

Have I completed the necessary research?

Stage 3:
Planning

Have I planned the essay?

Stage 4:
Writing

Have I written in the style required (analytical or factual)?

Is what I have written relevant to the title?

Is there a logical development and conclusion to the essay?

Are my facts and quotations accurate?

Stage 5:
Presentation

Have I quoted my sources?

Have I written enough?

Have I listed the books I have read, and referred to, in my bibliography?

Stage 6:
Checking

Is each major idea developed in a separate paragraph?

Have I avoided clichés, jargon & slang?

Have I checked carefully for mis-spellings?

Have I left any words out?

Have I used punctuation properly?

Have I kept a copy of the essay?

Stage 6 Checking

 After I've finished writing an essay I know I should check it through but for some reason I just want to hand it in as soon as possible. *'*

Many students are so relieved when they finish writing that they overlook checking, or persuade themselves it is not necessary. Some know they haven't done the essay title justice, and would be embarrassed to read it through.

In fact checking is quickly done and allows you to ensure that your essay is not marred by an obvious mistake, or made difficult to read by a slip of the pen.

Use the checklist on page 85 as a guide when writing and checking your essays.

Feedback

When their essays are returned too many students look only at the grade or mark, and not at the comment. To benefit from the process of marking you should take careful note of the marginal and final comments made on your essay. If there is something you do not understand then this is the best time to follow the question up.

It is valuable to note down separately the comments made on your essay, and then to make your own comment. Don't simply write "I must try harder" – that is too vague to be useful. Instead note one or two specific ways in which you could improve in your next essay.

By filling in the Feedback Record Sheet on page 87 you will be able to learn from your mistakes, and to monitor closely your own progress. This is particularly important if you are on a continuous assessment course.

RECORD SHEET

Feedback

Essay title and date	Marker's comments		My comments	

16 Widening your vocabulary

 I jot down words I'm not sure about, and then look them up later.

Why?

Broadening your vocabulary will

● Make you feel more self-confident in lessons and discussions
● Help you to follow the thread of a complex argument
● Enable you to select the shade of meaning you require
● Allow you to select words which are appropriate in particular contexts, for example in a formal or colloquial context.
● Improve your understanding of difficult books and articles
● Increase your reading speed because you won't have to stop to puzzle out words, or look them up in a dictionary
● Help you to avoid repetition in Writing

We can classify your vocabulary into two categories:
Active vocabulary: words that you know and use in a variety of circumstances
Passive vocabulary: words that you understand but would be unlikely to use.

In order to broaden your vocabulary you might transfer words from your passive to active vocabulary, and add words to your passive vocabulary.

Which words?

You will only learn new words effectively when you need to know them. This is how you learned to speak originally. You should concentrate, therefore, on

● words which will help your studies
● words that you meet in reading
● words you will be able to use in notes, essays and discussion

Trying to learn lists of words copied from a dictionary or a magazine is to remove the point and context from learning. This is frustrating, time wasting and pointless.

How?

Context

The context (the sentence or paragraph that a word is in) often provides clues to the meaning of an unfamiliar word. For example you may not know the meaning of 'antecedent' but when you read it you might be able to deduce part of the general sense of the word, though not its specific meaning:

> "The antecedent of this modern theory is to be found in an obscure book published in 1848."

The more frequently you meet a word in a variety of contexts the clearer you will become about its precise meaning and connotations.

Dictionaries

Look up unfamiliar words in a good modern dictionary. *Collins English Dictionary* is the best one volume dictionary, and is particularly good on scientific terms.

Personal dictionary

A couple of pages at the back of your file, or in your exercise book, can be effectively used to make your own dictionary. By rephrasing the dictionary definition, and by writing your own sentence containing the word, you will help to fix its meaning in your mind.

Thesaurus

A thesaurus can be useful if you are seeking
● a particular shade of meaning
● a word that has slipped your mind
● a word to suit a particular context
(See *Key reference books explained*, page 55)

Reading

Wide reading of books, and magazines such as the *New Statesman, New Scientist* and *New Society,* will help to broaden your vocabulary.

Glossaries

Many books which make use of technical terms contain a glossary to explain these words.

Active listening

Listening attentively in lessons, and to serious items on television and on the radio, will help you to become aware of how words are used.

FACT SHEET

Prefixes and suffixes

A prefix is a group of letters which when put at the front of a word, or word stem, changes the meaning. Suffixes are word endings. Knowing the meaning of some prefixes and suffixes will help you to deduce the general meaning of many words.

Below is a list of prefixes in alphabetical order. The meaning of each is given. Give an example of the use of each.

Prefix	Meaning	Example
Ab	away from, out, of	*abscond*
Ad	to	
Ante	before	
Auto	self, by one's self	
Bene	well	
Bi	two, twice	
Cata	below, down	
Co	together	
Com (or con)	together, with	
Contra	against	
De	below, down	
Dia	through, across	
Dis	apart, removal	
E	away from, out, of	
En	in, into, cause to be	
Epi	on	
Ex	away from, out, of	
Hetero	unlike	
Homo	same	
Hyper	over, in excess	
Hypo	below, down	
In	not	
Infra	below, beneath	
Inter	between, among, across, through	
Mis	wrong, ill	
Omni	all	
Ortho	straight, upright, true	
Palaeo	old, ancient, prehistoric	
Per	through, across, by means of	
Philo	love	
Poly	many	
Post	after	
Pre	before	
Pro	before, in front of	
Re	again, repeated	
Retro	backwards, after, behind	
Sub	below, under, part of	
Tele	far, distant	
Trans	across, through	

On a separate piece of paper you could now group these prefixes according to meaning, for example by listing those which mean down or below.

Certain suffixes indicate the function of words: – –tion = a noun
– –ly = an adverb
– –ful = an adjective

17 Dealing with data

 Like most people I need time to absorb information.

Data is presented in a variety of ways: you must be able to

- recognise the method of presentation
- appreciate any limitations this style might have
- extract the information you require
- compare information from two or more sources of data
- combine information from different sources
- draw conclusions
- make predictions (projections)
- present information in a way which emphasises any point you wish to make clear

The exercises which follow are designed to give you practice in these techniques. The data are all concerned with food.

Chart 1

Energy required as food (kilojoules [KJ]/Kilogram [Kg] bodyweight/day)

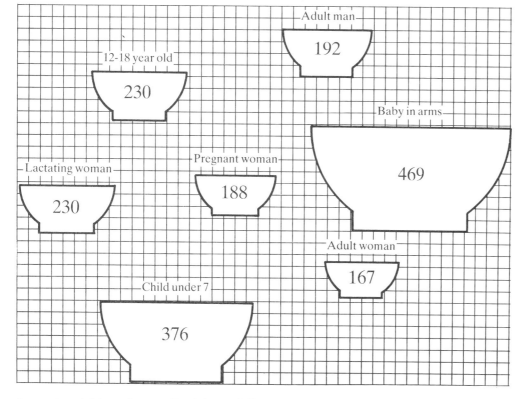

A growing child needs more food than a fully grown man.

TRUE or FALSE

Complete this table, then calculate if you are correct.

Table 1

	Energy from food KJ/Kg/day	Average weight Kg	Energy reqd. from food KJ/day
Adult man	192	70	13440 (70 × 192)
Adult woman			
Pregnant woman			
Lactating woman			
12-18 year old			
Child under 7			
Baby in arms			

An adult man requires 192 kilojoules (KJ) for every kilogram (Kg) of his body per day. If a man weighs 70 Kg he needs 192 × 70 KJ of energy every day. He must eat enough food to supply this energy.

The information contained in Chart 1 was not sufficient to answer the question posed. Moreover it required reorganisation to present it in a form which highlighted the answer.

Use Table 1 to calculate the **average daily energy required from food per person.**

Answer . . . . . KJ/Person/Day

Why is your answer not likely to be the same as the **average daily energy required from food per person** if a whole village, town or county is studied?

. . . .

. . . .

. . . .

. . . .

. . . .

Study this **bar chart**

Bar Chart 1

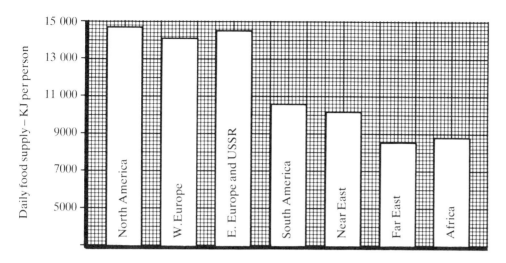

Draw a clear horizontal line on Bar Chart 1 to represent the **average daily energy required from food per person**. The average, worldwide, is calculated to be 10,000 KJ/person/day; your answer should have been in the range 9500–10,500 KJ/person/day.

The **critical limit** is the lowest possible energy supply which will keep someone alive. A person who is always completely at rest needs only 6700 KJ a day. This is the critical limit for humans. The lowness of this limit reflects our capacity for survival.

Draw a line on Bar Chart 1 to represent the 6700 KJ/person/day critical limit and label it clearly.

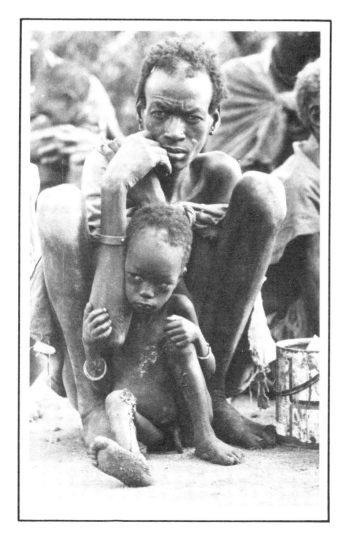

Below the critical limit.

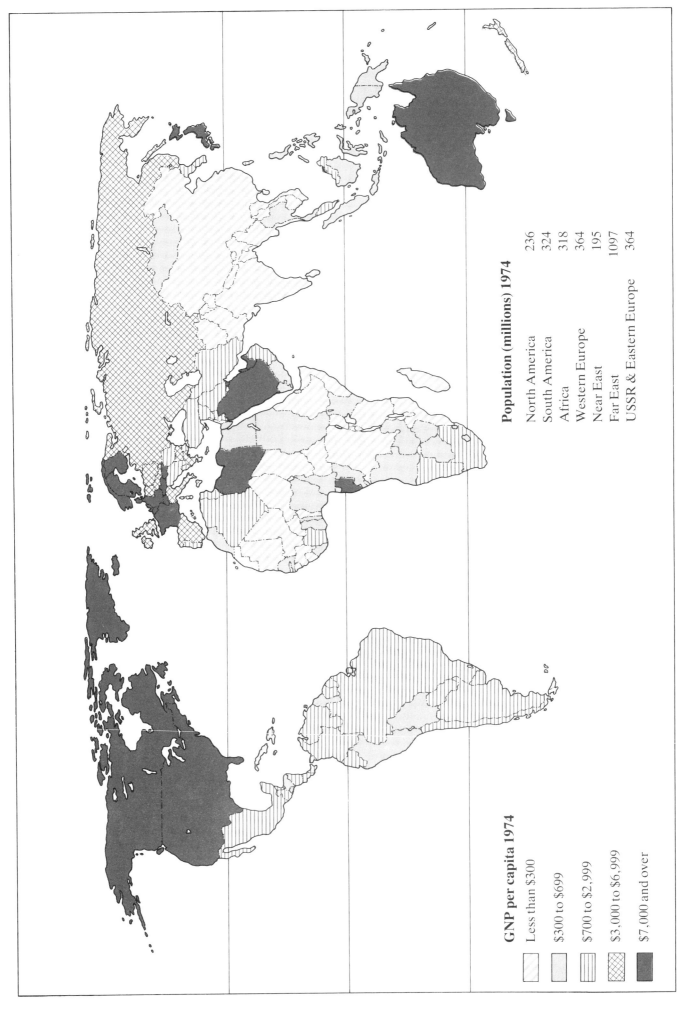

Population (millions) 1974

North America	236
South America	324
Africa	318
Western Europe	364
Near East	195
Far East	1097
USSR & Eastern Europe	364

GNP per capita 1974

Less than $300
$300 to $699
$700 to $2,999
$3,000 to $6,999
$7,000 and over

The population data on the world map on page 94 represent these areas:

Chart 2

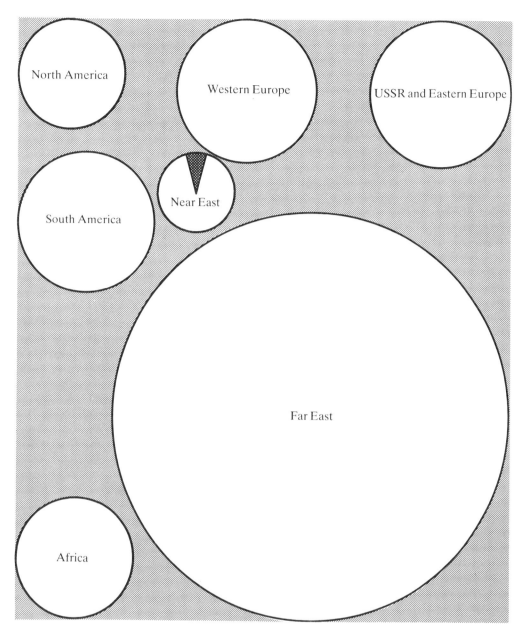

Key ▨ = Proportion of the population starving

Why are the circles different sizes?

. . . .

Study this bar chart.

Bar Chart 2

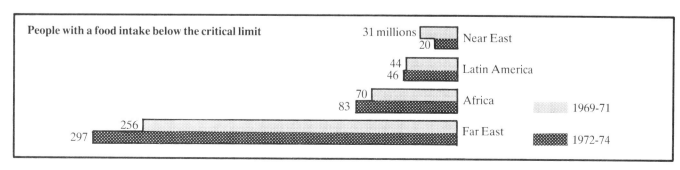

Suggest a way in which the data for the Near East (Arabia, Persian Gulf) is different from that of other regions

. . . .

. . . .

. . . .

Suggest a reason why the proportion on Bar Chart 2 in 1969/71 is greater than that for 1972/74 for the Near East.

. . . .

. . . .

. . . .

Use the data in Bar Chart 2 (1972-74) and the population figures from the world map to assess the proportion of starving people in the regions studied.

In the Near East in 1972-74, 20 million people were considered to be starving. The total population was 195 million people. Just over one in ten people were starving, therefore, a one tenth segment of the circle in Chart 2 (36° since it is a tenth of a full circle) has been shaded in.

Now complete the exercise for the other regions shown in Bar Chart 2 on page 95.

The Gross National Product (GNP) of a country is its claimed yearly output. The value of the GNP is converted to US $ to make comparison between countries possible.

Compare the GNP data shown on the map to the data now shown in Chart 2.

Write down your conclusions.

. . . .

. . . .

. . . .

. . . .

. . . .

. . . .

Present this comparison in a diagrammatic way which emphasises your conclusion.

Study this Histogram (A) and Line Graph (B) of agricultural exports.

Value of Agricultural Exports 1971-77 (US $ millions)

A

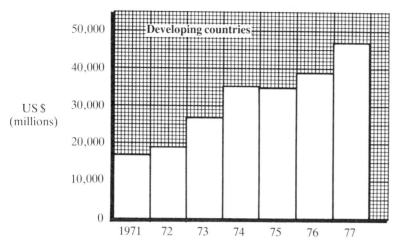

Do you notice the difference between a bar chart and a histogram?
The data that is compared on a bar chart is separate. The data on a histogram is continuous.
Compare Bar Chart 1 to the Histogram (A)

B

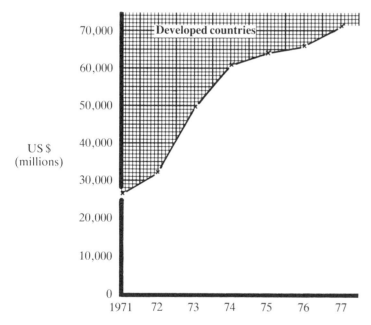

Use this data to calculate the proportion of world trade in agriculture in 1971 and 1977 for developing and developed countries. Complete Table 2.

Table 2

Proportion of World Trade in Agriculture (US $ Millions)

	Developing countries	Developed countries
1971		
1977		

What does this mean for the developing countries?

. . . .

. . . .

We have considered only agricultural world trade. When industrial business is included as well as finance and insurance, is the situation of the developing countries better or worse?

. . . .

. . . .

How does the graph below explain the flattening of both the Histogram (A) and Graph (B)?

. . . .

. . . .

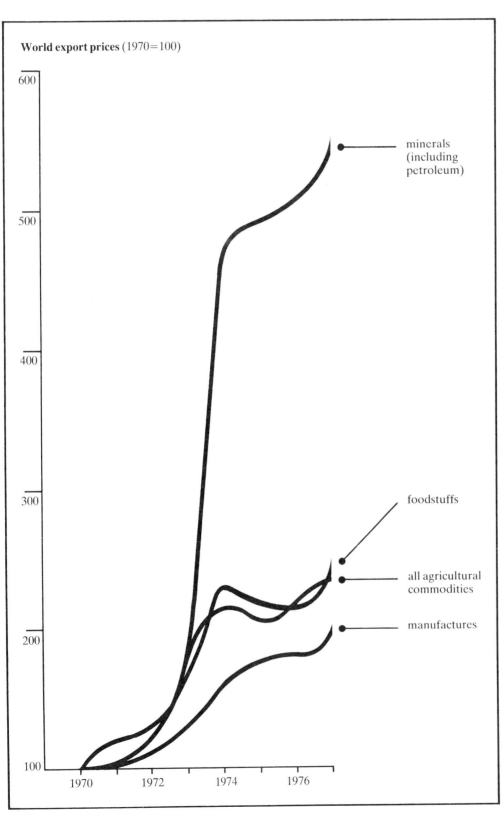

This type of scale is an "index".

In 1970 the World Export Prices were calculated and set to a scale where their value at the time equalled 100.

The Financial Times and the American Dow Jones indexes were once also set at 100.
What are they now?

. . . .

18 Making use of computers

> ' *Once you've mastered it the computer is very useful for working with graphs and statistics.* '

> ' *I use the computer sometimes, but usually just as a gimmick. A notebook is far handier.* '

> ' *I find a wordprocessor a superb aid in writing essays. I still make a plan on paper but then, instead of having to write, re-draft and finally produce a best copy, I can type the essay into the computer, rearrange, add, delete and correct until I'm satisfied.* '

To appreciate how to use computers in your study you need to understand some simple terminology.

Computers exist in many forms, from microcomputers to large mainframe computer systems which occupy many rooms. Every computer needs a set of instructions to tell it what to do. This set of instructions is known as a **program**. The **programs** that are referred to as software are written in a **language** which the particular computer can understand.

There are hundreds of computer languages, each with certain characteristics which make it suitable for a particular task. For study purposes the more important languages are:

BASIC, LOGO, PILOT, COMAL and PROLOG

You do not need to know these languages in order to use a computer.

There are three main areas in which computers can help you to learn and aid your study:

1 as an administrative aid to direct and control what you learn;
2 as a wordprocessor;
3 to assist you in learning.

Administrative aid
Databases

A database is a collection of data items about a particular topic or topics that can be interrogated by the user to obtain information. Databases are very important because they allow information to be extracted easily and rapidly. Databases are commonly used as indexes to:

● Books and periodicals in a library
● Abstracts (summaries) from technical journals.

In these two cases, the databases do not contain the information you seek but provide you with the means for finding it.

Consider the following tasks:

Case 1 Finding the titles and Dewey numbers of all the books written by a particular author.

Case 2 Compiling a list of all the books concerned with *Computers in Education* published since 1975.

Case 3 Compiling a list of references to articles on a particular topic, published in a specialist journal since 1960.

All these tasks can be carried out on existing databases. But, what are the advantages of using a database?

Case 1

You could go to a conventional catalogue to do this and the time taken would be almost the same as using a computer. If your author has a common name, such as Smith, you will waste much time in having to scan many irrelevant cards in the catalogue. A good database would allow you to pinpoint precisely the sorts of books you are looking for quickly and easily.

Case 2

This would be a very time consuming task. You would have to match all the book references to *Computers* with those of *Education* and identify those books which are in both lists. The database could provide you with this information instantaneously.

Case 3

This situation would at the very least require you to read the list of contents of each issue of the journal since 1960. A well structured database should give you the information you require in a matter of minutes or even seconds.

Summary

Databases are capable of accessing vast amounts of information very quickly and sifting out the facts that you require. They do this by looking for keywords and cross referencing. If you ask the right question **in the right way** you will get the answer you require. Databases are capable of performing very quickly tasks that would otherwise take you a long time. More importantly they can perform tasks that you would otherwise not consider worthwhile. Ask at your local Library to see what database facilities they provide.

You have probably seen data contained in databases without even realising it, on your television set.

TELETEXT

Both BBC and ITV provide access to databases for the general public. These databases are known as CEEFAX and ORACLE and generically as TELETEXT. Whenever television programmes are being transmitted so are pages (screen fulls) of information about **sport, travel, weather, news** and so on. Special adapters can be purchased to attach to your television or home computer to enable you to receive this information.

PRESTEL

Another system available to the general public in Britain is British Telecom's PRESTEL. As with TELETEXT the information is supplied by companies, educational establishments and public service organisations. A user needs to buy an adapter for his television or computer **and** a telephone.

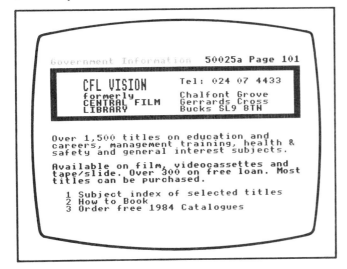

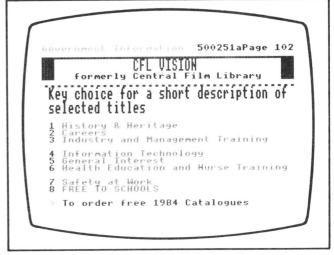

PRESTEL differs from TELETEXT because it allows the user to send messages via the telephone to the computer. In this way the user can request information and be sent a reply if needed. Users can also send messages to other users. There are many other databases being created for the public to access, which operate in a similar way to PRESTEL.

Both TELETEXT and PRESTEL allow the user to download software, that is, to transfer the transmitted information into the computer. This software can then be saved on a disc and used at a later date.

Wordprocessors

Some people think of a wordprocessor as a glorified typewriter but it is much more than that. It can either be a dedicated machine bought specifically as a wordprocessor or it can be a computer with a program to make it act as a wordprocessor. A wordprocessor usually comprises a keyboard, a screen on which to view your work, a disc drive or cassette to enable you to save your work and retrieve it later and a printer on which to reproduce your work on paper.

You don't need to be typist to use a wordprocessor. Below is a brief summary of what you can do with it.

● Enter your written information via the keyboard.
● Easily and quickly correct spelling or typing errors.
● Review it on the screen before printing it.
● Instantly rearrange the order of words, sentences and paragraphs.
● Save your information and come back to it later to revise and update it.
● Print it.
● A wordprocessor provides you with many facilities such as automatic page numbering, the ability to change tense or to change from capitals to small letters, underlining, searching and replacing words or phrases.

How can it help you?

● It will enable you to present information neatly and in a suitable layout.
● You will be able to make necessary alterations or updates and immediately obtain a new copy without having to retype everything.
● You can re-arrange, redraft or reorganise creative writing or essays without the chore of rewriting.
● You can print extra copies with ease.
● You can even purchase a program that will automatically check your spellings.

Wordprocessor work station

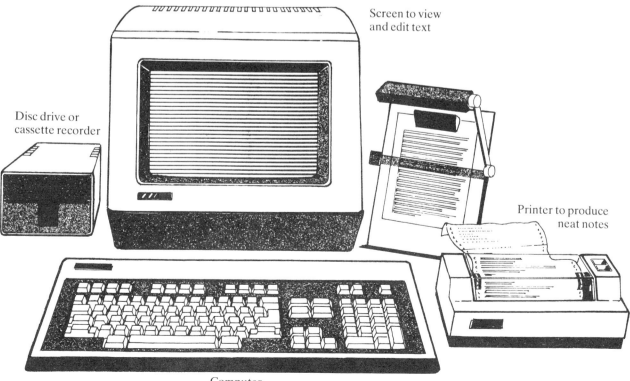

Screen to view and edit text

Disc drive or cassette recorder

Printer to produce neat notes

Computer

To assist you in learning

Computers are now used extensively in schools and colleges and apart from their obvious use in Computer Studies departments they are used in the teaching of many other subjects. This use of computers for teaching is often known as CAL (Computer Assisted Learning). The main principle of using computers in learning is to enable the student to gain an insight into a specific topic that he or she could not gain using conventional methods.

You may be familiar with programmed learning; you read a page or a frame and then a question is posed. If you answer correctly you move on to the next piece of work or possibly another question. If your answer was incorrect you are directed to a revision frame, followed by another question. When you prove yourself to be proficient in the area under study the next frame is presented to you. The same idea is employed by computers that can handle this technique very effectively and add another dimension. They present interesting and varied information which can be animation, text, charts, or diagrams or any combination of these. The computer can make assessments of your progress and can make decisions on what it shows you or asks you next, as a result of your response. Thus it can pinpoint shortcomings in your understanding. Remember though, that in assisting you in your learning, the computer is only as good as the software you use.

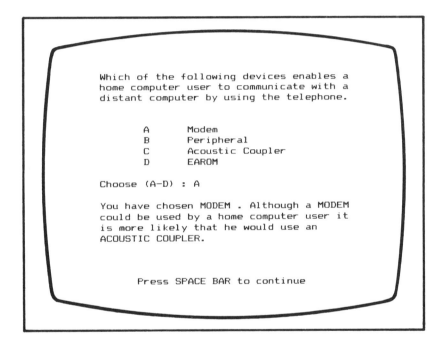

Computers make good learning aids because they have the ability to:

● Work very quickly
● Produce diagrams and charts
● Animate the pictures
● Repeat monotonous procedures over and over again without becoming bored or inconsistent.

Computer programs for education usually fall into one of the following categories.

● Information handling
● Structured reinforcement
● Modelling and simulation
● Games and Role play

Information handling

We have already dealt in detail with this section. It involves the use of wordprocessors and databases for retrieving information that has been stored by yourself or others. Modern microprocessor systems usually have software which will allow users to create their own database. This can be very useful if you need to collate a lot of data and extract information in different ways. Information handling also involves the use of information systems such as TELETEXT or PRESTEL.

Structured reinforcement

This usually concerns the learning of facts or information through repetition. For example, you might use this in learning spelling or French vocabulary or the Periodic Table etc.

Modelling and simulation

A simulation is a representation on a computer of a physical situation. Its main purpose is to give the student experience of interacting with something that in the real world would be dangerous, time consuming, or difficult. Examples would be:

● Transpiration of water molecules from the surface of a leaf, which it is not possible to see.
● The internal operation of a nuclear power station reactor, which it would be dangerous to see.
● The rate of soil erosion from a hillside, which happens over many years.

Such simulations usually allow the user to alter factors, observe the effect and make further changes. In some you might be asked to make judgements and enter your decisions into the computer and then observe the outcome. In this way you can see at first hand the effect of your decisions on the model and test theories. A book can only give one version whereas the computer program can pose questions such as: '. . . what would happen if?'. Conversely the user, by changing parameters (factors) and getting the computer to respond, can investigate the model in a way which he or she could not do otherwise.

Games and role play

Programs in this category usually enable individuals or groups to become involved in a situation in which each person's actions affects what is happening to others. Many programs in this category have been written for economics for the teaching of such topics as:

● Supply and Demand
● Running the British Economy

Below is an example of a typical program designed to let students experiment with the British Economy. It is interesting to note that even the Government uses programs written on the same lines to test their economic theories before putting them into practice. A word of warning here, 'the program is only as good as the underlying model'. If the model is faulty then the predictions will be too. Many governments have found this out to their cost. It is easy, for example, to write a program to make predictions, it is far more difficult to make predictions that will come true.

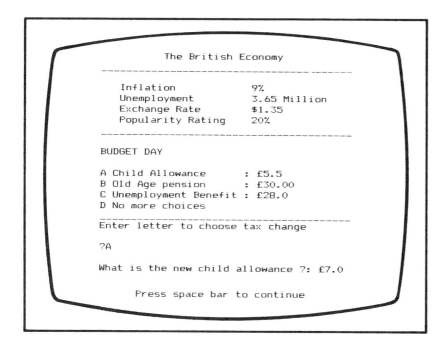

```
              The British Economy
  ------------------------------------- -------

      Inflation          9%
      Unemployment       3.65 Million
      Exchange Rate      $1.35
      Popularity Rating  20%
  -------------------------------------
  BUDGET DAY

  A Child Allowance    : £5.5
  B Old Age pension    : £30.00
  C Unemployment Benefit : £28.0
  D No more choices
  -------------------------------------
  Enter letter to choose tax change

  ?A

  What is the new child allowance ?: £7.0

         Press space bar to continue
```

How to choose a computer

There are many computers on the market which are designed to be used at home. All microcomputers however will not do all the tasks outlined above. It is necessary before buying a computer, to decide what you want to do with it and then to try and find the machine that will fulfil all or most of your needs. Here are some questions to bear in mind.

1 Will it be used as a wordprocessor? If so, does it have a proper keyboard and are there suitable programs that will make it operate as a wordprocessor?
2 Does it have facilities for connecting it to the telephone system or other computers?
3 Can you connect a disk drive and printer to it?
4 **Most importantly** is there a large amount of **good** software available which you would find useful?

There are a number of microcomputers available which fulfil many of the above criteria (at the time of writing). The technology changes very rapidly though, and new computers combining different functions will continue to become available in the years ahead.

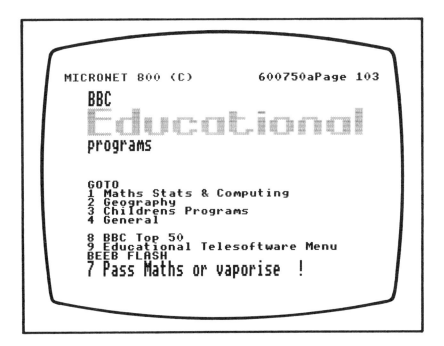

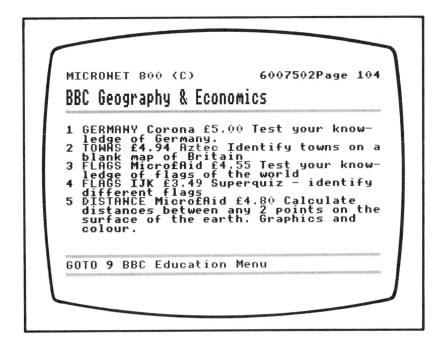

19 Revision

' A file full of notes is daunting so condense it into very succinct notes and headings. '

' Revise more on your weaker subjects. '

' Don't listen to what your friends say about the amount of revising they've done or not done. '

' You can't revise what you don't understand. '

' Planning a revision programme makes me feel less nervous and more organised. '

Regular reviewing

Revision can be very demanding of your time and energy. Your enthusiasm for your subject can be stretched to the limit, but the stress can be taken out of revision by regularly reviewing your work throughout the year. Examinations set out to measure how well you can remember, understand and apply what you know. Whilst revision aids recall, understanding and application are continuous processes. Revision helps a student to see the course in perspective but waiting until the end of the course for this overview is clearly not the best way to study.

Regular reviewing is an efficient, effective and rewarding way to revise. Reviewing involves going over notes, essays, tests and questions at regular intervals. Reviewing is discussed on page 31. You are recommended to use this technique in particular to prepare yourself for examinations; it is by far the most successful method.

Use the study year planner

Regular reviewing should be built into your study timetable.

Revision

The final preparation for examinations

There are four stages of revision:
1. Preparing your study material
2. Assessing your progress
3. Preparing a revision timetable
4. Using a variety of revision strategies

1 Preparing your study material

If you are taking examinations in June use the Christmas holiday to get your study materials organised. Bring your notes up to date; your fellow students will be more willing to loan you their notes now than at any time from now on!

Check the accuracy of your notes, make sure any ideas which you don't understand are investigated. Learning is almost impossible without understanding and appreciating patterns and structure in the work. Refer to recommended books and your fellow students to help you with any sections of work you are uncertain about. In January discuss any remaining problems with your teacher or tutor.

Take special note of comments your teachers make about your work, see *Feedback*, page 87. Draw up your own feedback sheet, it is an excellent way of recording your strengths as well as weaknesses.

Summary
● Complete your notes
● Correct mistakes
● Clarify misconceptions
● Check over teachers' comments
● Improve weaker work

2 Assessing your progress

Make a fresh assessment of how well your studies are going. It is important you start your final preparations with an honest and realistic appreciation of your strengths and weaknesses as well as any hindrances which prevent effective study. Rate your progress by completing a *Self Assessment Profile*, page 34.

Now make a general comment on your progress.

. . . .

. . . .

. . . .

3 Preparing a revision timetable

A major part of the Easter break should be reserved for revision. About 6-8 weeks prior to exams your revision schedule should take shape. Allocate a definite part of every day for drafting revision notes, see page 43. Aim to have a full set of these notes before your course resumes. They will allow you to make the most of any revision period your tutor has set aside.

Fill in a planner (page 15) for each week before the exam. Revision will make great demands on your free time but don't underestimate the importance of relaxation. Exercise makes a good break. Study sessions of less than 15 minutes are of little value as are those of more than one hour. A block of three hours might be broken up into 3 sessions, each lasting 40-50 minutes with a good break between sessions, see page 27.

Work out how many sessions you can devote to each subject and, by using your notes or the syllabus, allocate topics to study sessions. Plan to revise all topics, bearing in mind that extra time will be needed for

● special subjects/studies
● weaker subjects/topics
● regular reviewing, which is still necessary

Try to cover a variety of topics in any one block of time and avoid devoting consecutive sessions to the same subject. Alternate those topics you enjoy with those you find difficult or boring.

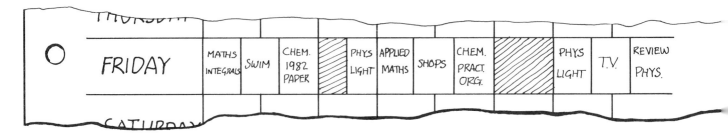

When you have developed your schedule consider which strategies you should use. Make use of a variety of strategies. Review your schedule after a couple of weeks modifying any aspects if necessary. Reappraisal of your schedule and strategies can be a worthwhile exercise leading to more effective revision, but the temptation to change your plans on more than a couple of occasions should be resisted.

In the period immediately before exams, when you feel under most pressure to revise, avoid working long and late hours. It is in this period when you can reap the benefits of regular reviewing and a well thought out and implemented revision plan. You should be mentally and physically fresh for the examination; a tired, anxious candidate is at an obvious disadvantage.

4 Using a variety of revision strategies

Use the range of strategies outlined below, and any others that suit you and your subject, to make your revision as interesting and effective as possible.

Revision strategies

Making revision notes

Writing notes has helped you to understand and learn your subject. Writing revision notes will refresh your memory on details and simultaneously give you a broader picture of your studies. The notes you are redrafting will be on familiar work and an active learner will look for more details and try to understand the less obvious ideas. The familiarity of the work means revision notes can be much more concise; if you need more detail you can refer to your original notes.

Writing revision notes helps to keep your mind on the task of revising and compels you to think about what you are writing. Simply by reducing the volume of notes you are distinguishing between important ideas and supporting detail. This selection and rejection also involves you in structuring your revision notes in order to show the links between ideas. After redrafting your notes you will have a compact aid which will be perfect for last minute revision. Before you start to redraft your notes read *Making Notes,* page 35, which contains a section on revising from notes. Consider writing condensed linear notes and making a pattern note of a group of related topics. Two chemistry students, for example, used two approaches to the same topic: the first used pattern note summaries, the second chose to break up the topic and put each subsection on a record card.

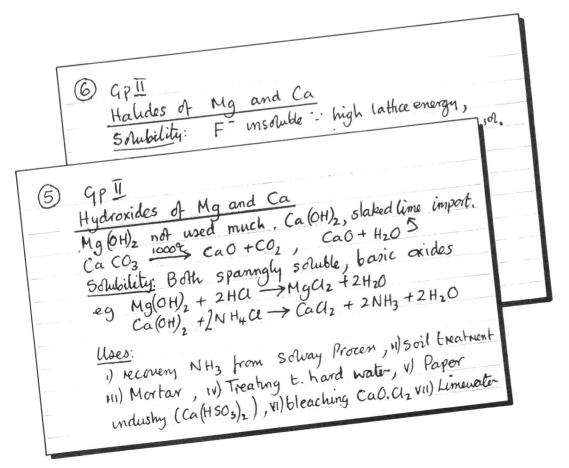

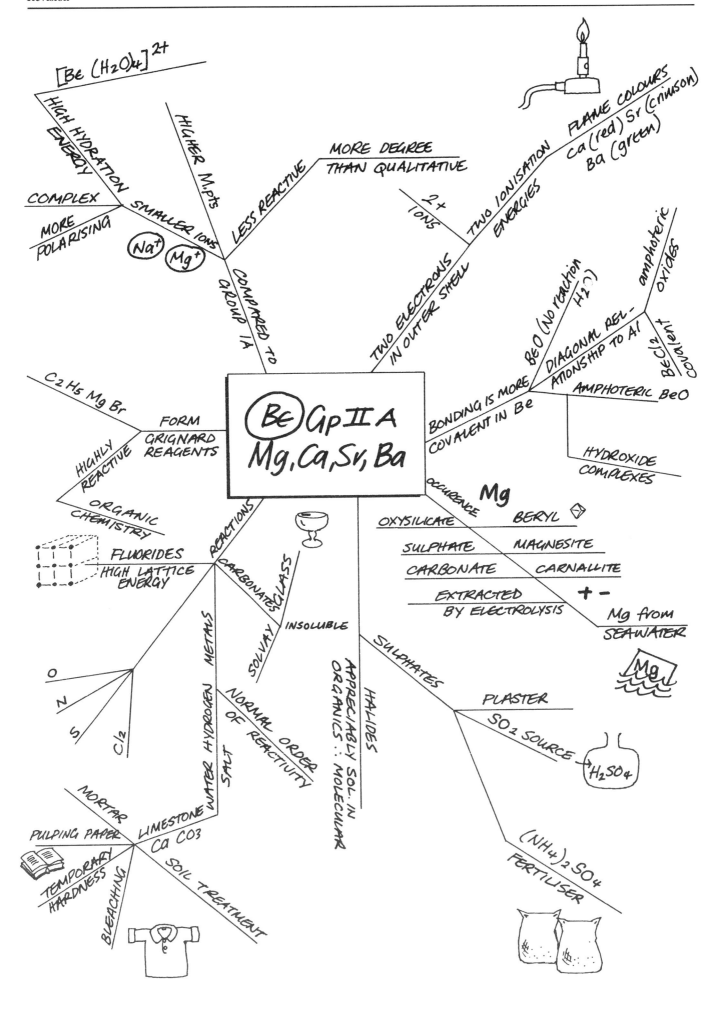

$[Be(H_2O)_4]^{2+}$

HIGH HYDRATION ENERGY

COMPLEX

MORE POLARISING

SMALLER IONS

Na^+ Mg^+

HIGHER M.pts

LESS REACTIVE

COMPARED TO GROUP 1A

MORE DEGREE THAN QUALITATIVE

$2+$ IONS

TWO ELECTRONS IN OUTER SHELL

TWO IONISATION ENERGIES

FLAME COLOURS
Ca (red) Sr (crimson)
Ba (green)

BeO (No reaction H_2O)

DIAGONAL RELATIONSHIP TO Al

amphoteric oxides

$BeCl_2$ covalent

BONDING IS MORE COVALENT IN Be

AMPHOTERIC BeO

HYDROXIDE COMPLEXES

Be Gp II A
Mg, Ca, Sr, Ba

C_2H_5MgBr

FORM GRIGNARD REAGENTS

HIGHLY REACTIVE

ORGANIC CHEMISTRY

FLUORIDES
HIGH LATTICE ENERGY

REACTIONS

CARBONATES

SOLVAY LASS

INSOLUBLE

Mg

OCCURRENCE

OXYSILICATE   BERYL

SULPHATE   MAGNESITE

CARBONATE   CARNALLITE

EXTRACTED BY ELECTROLYSIS

$+$ $-$

Mg from SEAWATER

METALS

HYDROGEN

WATER

SALT

NORMAL ORDER OF REACTIVITY

O

N

S

Cl_2

HALIDES
APPRECIABLY SOL. IN ORGANICS ∴ MOLECULAR

SULPHATES

PLASTER

SO_2 SOURCE

H_2SO_4

MORTAR

PULPING PAPER

LIMESTONE $CaCO_3$

TEMPORARY HARDNESS

BLEACHING

SOIL TREATMENT

$(NH_4)_2SO_4$
FERTILISER

Reading notes

Reading notes as a method of revision must be an active process. Passive reading can be avoided by using some of the strategies mentioned in the chapter on *Reading,* page 56.

Try writing down the **key words** in a section and, when you have finished, reconstruct the main ideas using the key words. Sketch diagrams, graphs and charts on scrap paper. Mark very important details with a highlighter pen.

Using examination papers

Besides making you familiar with the type of questions which you are likely to meet, working through previous exam papers offers the opportunity to gauge how well you are learning your work. During your course you are likely to have tackled many exam questions. You probably used your notes and text books to produce your best answer, this being a good way of consolidating your learning. At revision time you should use no aids whatsoever. Prepare yourself for the question by reading your notes. Answer the question to the best of your ability. After a break use your notes to mark your answer. Be scrupulous in dealing with every point, aim to improve it before moving on to the next question.

Some students create a bank of model or specimen answers to questions, the value of this exercise varies from subject to subject. Take care not to become too involved in question spotting if you use this method. Writing and marking exam answers will show up your strengths and weaknesses, and will help you to choose questions.

Remembering

Part of the revision programme will be devoted to remembering the factual content of your course. Testing recall only can be achieved in a few simple ways.

● Answering exam questions under exam conditions
● Writing out sections that have to be learned
● Speaking (perhaps recording) sections which have to be learned
● Ask others to question you (using your notes)
● Try teaching someone else. This is an excellent, but slow, way of revising
● Try modelling your notes by transposing your notes from written to diagrammatic form and vice versa

20 Exam skills

' *As they say when hitch-hiking round the Galaxy, "Don't panic".* '

' *Think and never regurgitate facts.* '

' *Don't be too calm and relaxed. Keep alert and slightly nervous. That way you should work quickly and well.* '

' *Do not twist the question to what you wish to write about.* '

' *Don't write all you know on a topic – the examiner wants to know if you understand and can discuss a subject.* '

' *Be concise and precise. Read the question very carefully before you start. Think carefully before you write.* '

' *Divide your time according to the number of marks for each question.* '

The year before

Past papers

Look at past exam papers (make sure they are the right ones) to familiarise yourself with the type of questions you will be asked, and the structure of the exam.

Key question words

Make sure you understand what different key question words mean:

Keywords O—🔑 explained

Compare:	Are the things very alike (similar) or are there important differences? Which do you think is best? Why?
Contrast:	Look for differences.
Criticise:	Use evidence to support your opinion on the value or merit of theories, facts or views of others.
Define:	Give the meaning.
Describe:	Write in detail.
Differentiate:	Explain the difference.
Discuss:	Write about the important aspects of the topic, are there two sides to the question? Consider the arguments for and against.
Distinguish:	Explain the difference.
Evaluate:	Judge the importance or success.
Explain:	Make clear.
Illustrate:	Give examples which make the point clear.
Interpret:	Explain the meaning in your own words, for example you may be asked to interpret a graph.

Justify: Give reasons to support an argument or action.
Outline: Choose the most important aspects of a topic. Ignore the minor detail.
Relate: Show the connection between things.
State: Write briefly the main point.
Summarise: Bring together the main points.
Trace: Show how something has developed from beginning to end.

The exam instructions (The rubric)

Find out exactly how many questions you have to answer. Are any questions compulsory? Must you answer questions from every section?

Timing

Exactly how long is the exam? Take note of the number of marks for each section, then calculate how much time you have for each question. Allow time for selecting questions, and for checking at the end of the exam.

Equipment

What are you allowed to take into the exam with you?

Mock exams

The mocks allow you to discover

a   weaknesses in your subject knowledge
b   how effective your study skills, in particular your revision and exam technique, are
c   what are your strengths and weaknesses when working under pressure

After the mocks you should assess your performance honestly. See *Study Profile*, page 34.

Write down what changes you will need to make to prepare yourself for the actual exams. By giving equal attention to your teachers' comments as well as your marks you will minimise last minute nerves and doubts.

Immediately before

The night before

Set out everything you need, such as spare pens and pencils, so as to avoid a rush in the morning.

Some students prefer to take a complete break the night before, but most people do some last minute revising. By briefly reviewing the main points in your notes you can prepare yourself mentally.

The exam day

Get to the exam room early. If you have to rush you will not be in the best frame of mind for a three hour paper.

In the exam

Choosing your questions

Scan all the questions and tick any ones you could answer. Read these questions carefully – it is easy to misread titles under the pressure of the moment. Every year examiners report that thousands of candidates penalise themselves by not answering the question set or by answering an incorrect number of questions.

Planning

- Underline the key words in the question to focus your attention on exactly what you are being asked.
- In essay writing ask yourself does the title require an analytical or factual essay.
- Ask yourself does the title provide a structure for your answer.
- Planning gives you the opportunity to demonstrate to the examiner that you can make decisions on priorities, allocating the greatest attention to the most relevant parts.
- Planning helps you to write your answer in a coherent way.
- Planning gives you confidence during the exam, helps you to think clearly and makes you feel calmer when you are writing.
- Planning prevents you repeating yourself, or writing too much or too little.

Timing

Divide your time carefully between the number of questions you have to answer, and stick to your time limits. Marks are allocated for valid points made in an answer. For some exams there is a detailed marking scheme of points which the examiners are looking for. Marks are not gained by writing at great length.

It is essential to answer the required number of questions in order to do your best in the exam. Look at the example below of two students of comparable ability: Student A answers three questions at some length but has not left time even to begin question four; Student B completes the whole paper. Note the difference in their exam performance.

Question	Student A's marks	Student B's marks	Possible marks
1	15	13	25
2	14	11	25
3	12	11	25
4	0	12	25
Total	41	47	100

Writing an exam essay

Many students, particularly those who haven't developed the habit of planning an essay, go into excessive and often irrelevant detail in answering a question. The examiner needs to find a sense of direction in the essay to award marks. Too often examiners are left unsure of where they are going or when they have arrived.

Answer your best questions first but don't get carried away and try to impress the examiner with irrelevant information. There are no extra marks for answering questions which weren't set.

As you write keep referring back to the question and to your plan.

Concluding an essay

If you wish you can summarise your argument, but try not to repeat what you have already said. Avoid a crude concluding generalisation as if all along the question required only a single sentence answer beginning with the exam cliché "Thus it can be seen . . ."

If you do write a conclusion try to save some new point for this last paragraph, or some fresh viewpoint on the question.

Presentation

- Write legibly
- Keep your work as neat as possible
- Begin your paragraphs about 5 letters in from the margin
- Number your answers (and any subsections) clearly
- Keep quotes brief and to the point. Direct quotes should be in quotation marks.
- It is a waste of time to write an essay in rough and then copy it out again.
- Graphs, diagrams and tables should:
  1 be as accurate as possible
  2 be clearly labelled
  3 show their purpose
- In mathematical working the sequence of operations in an answer must be clear. Marks are awarded for logical deduction as well as for correct final answers.

Checking

Make sure errors are clearly corrected or deleted. Rough work should be clearly crossed out.

Summary: Think then write

21 How your brain works: Additional information

The structure of the brain

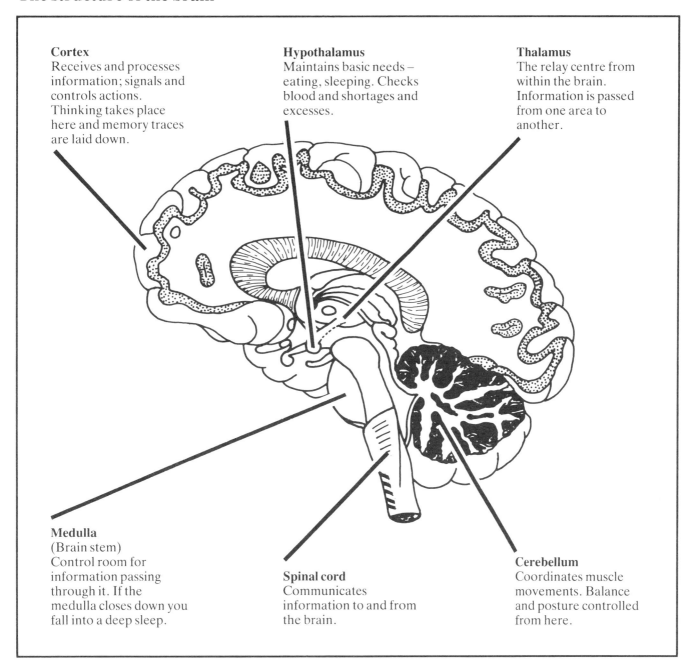

Cortex
Receives and processes information; signals and controls actions. Thinking takes place here and memory traces are laid down.

Hypothalamus
Maintains basic needs – eating, sleeping. Checks blood and shortages and excesses.

Thalamus
The relay centre from within the brain. Information is passed from one area to another.

Medulla
(Brain stem)
Control room for information passing through it. If the medulla closes down you fall into a deep sleep.

Spinal cord
Communicates information to and from the brain.

Cerebellum
Coordinates muscle movements. Balance and posture controlled from here.

The brain consumes a quarter of the oxygen we take into our blood to synthesise the protein required during thinking. The oxygen is supplied through membranes which surround the brain.

Using your brain

Few students understand the basic functions of the brain or how to make the most of it. The notion that our brain functions like a computer is true only at the most basic level of comparison. A computer works in a linear fashion, and can call upon terrific resources of memory. The brain is capable of operating in a linear and multi-dimensional way as a continuous processor of information of many different types and sources.

Our brain has the capacity to link streams of incoming information in a very complex way and to produce a new impression of the information; in other words the brain can synthesise as it works.

Research indicates only 0.1% of our brain's capacity is used. There is also evidence to support the idea that we never forget; everything we ever experience is recorded in the brain.

Of course we don't remember everything and it is important to distinguish between memory and remembering. If you were asked to name a few friends from your second year at school you could probably name one or two, and would then assume you had forgotten the rest. If a school photograph was produced some of the other names would spring to mind. Details like your classroom layout, and activities you were involved in, all help to re-establish your mental set and refresh your memory.

The brain thrives on use. A varied and rich environment, especially in the early years of life, considerably enhances the capacity for many operations.

Brain cells

All our brain cells are with us when we are born. A tiny fraction of these cells die as we get older and are not replaced. However, we learn to use our brain more effectively as we get older and its capacity continues to increase. Since it is estimated that we use only 0.1% of our brain it would take a very rapid decay to affect our performance.

The cells in the brain are of two main types:

Neurones
(Nerve cells)
These are 'action' cells used for remembering, thinking, controlling organs and muscles. There are 10 billion of them.

Glia cells
There are ten times as many glia cells as neurones. These are packed between neurones and insulate them from one another. They also service the neurones, provide nourishment and remove waste. They hold the brain together.

Neurones

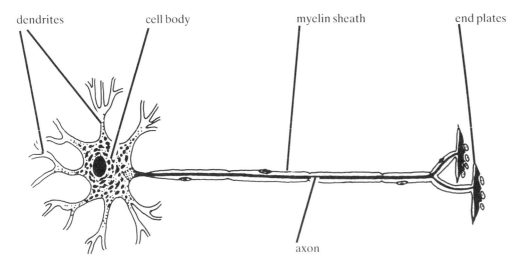

The dendrites link to other neurones and pass information to them. The information is received in the form of electrical impulses or chemicals and is passed down the axon and relayed to another neurone through the end plates. The neurones are linked in this way to form a vast network.

As we experience things and learn, inter-neurone connections form, and the extent and complexity of the network is a measure of the development of the brain.

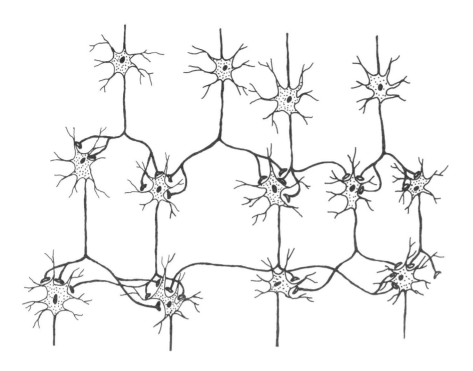

The synapse

A most important part of the system is the place where the end plates from one cell meet the dendrite from another. This 'connection' is called a synapse. Sometimes there is a direct electrical contact across the synapse but often there is not, and the minute gap between axon and dendrite is the control over whether a pulse of information is passed between neurones. Each particular experience causes a specific trace of electrical activity through the network of neurones. Remembering this experience means reactivating this trace. The trace of electrical activity, the pattern of activated neurones, remains specific because some synapse junctions stop electricity flowing. The synapse is of obvious importance in thinking and memory.

Chemicals play an active role in the transmission of signals across the synaptic gap. Some allow further transmission of the signal and some inhibit it. These chemicals appear to come from the cell body and move down the axon. They must also be important in learning and memory.

Memory

Large parts of the cortex become active when certain learning and remembering processes are taking place. It is known that at the same time there is appreciable protein synthesis.

When a neurone is activated by an electrical pulse, some chemicals, which are made in the cell body, move down the axon. It is these chemicals, which are proteins, that control the synapse. If certain chemicals are present at the synapse the electrical impulse is passed on to the next neurone otherwise it terminates at the synapse. By this method an electrical pattern, which results from some learning, can become permanently encoded onto the cortex. The electrical pattern which is the **short term memory,** is consolidated into a **long term memory** as a result of chemical changes at the synapse.

When the memory is recalled the encoded pathway is stimulated and the pattern of electrical activity recognised. By this theory we can appreciate the transient nature of short term memory.

There is experimental evidence from animal research that each memory or piece of learned behaviour has a specific chemical associated with it. These chemicals are also proteins and may encode a synapse. It has been possible to teach an animal certain behaviour and to extract and refine the chemical which was thought to have arisen from the learning. By transferring the chemical to the brain of another animal the behaviour was also transferred.

Jedidiah Buxton was born around 1707 in Derbyshire; he never learned to read or write and remained a farm labourer throughout his life. He was once asked "how many cubic yards of earth must be removed to make a pond 426ft long, 263ft wide and 2ft 6″ deep?" He answered correctly in 15 minutes!

George Bidder, a Devonian, was once asked "If a coachwheel was 5ft 10″ in circumference how many times would it revolve in 800,000,000 miles?" He gave the answer 724,114,285,704 (with 20 inches remaining!) in 15 seconds!

Playing a game of chess blindfolded is difficult enough but in 1960 the Belgian Master Koltanovski took on 56 opponents simultaneously. He won 50 games and drew 6.

22 Glossary

Analytical writing requires you to comment on a subject. See page 72.

Bar charts use columns on a graph to show differences in data. The information on the *x*-axis is already in separate groups, e.g. political parties in an opinion poll.

Bibliography: a list of books referred to in writing an essay. List the library code number, author, title and date of publication. See pages 57 and 84.

Blurb: the information on the back of a book. See page 56.

Classified catalogue: a complete list of a library's holdings arranged in numerical order according to classification (code) numbers. See page 50.

Flow chart: a diagrammatic representation of a process showing clearly how any one part relates to the whole.

Histogram: columns on a chart are used to show changes in frequency. The information on the *x*-axis is continuous, e.g. km per litre figures for cars at different speeds.

Key words: those words that are most loaded with meaning. See page 38.

Linear notes: traditional notes written in sentences and paragraphs, cf. *pattern note*.

Long term memory: the permanent storage of information in the brain.

Mental set: a state of mind when both conscious and subconscious attention is focussed on one particular activity. See page 18.

Mnemonics: memory aids to link information you want to recall by rhyme, mental picture or memorable sentence, e.g. the colours of the spectrum are contained in the sentence "Richard (red) of (orange) York (yellow) gave (green) battle (blue) in (indigo) vain (violet)".

Modelling: making a diagrammatic representation of information in a passage.

Overlearning: learning something so thoroughly that it becomes unforgettable.

Pattern note: a visually appealing way of presenting your knowledge about a topic, and of showing the important links between different aspects of the subject. Pattern notes are especially useful for summarising. See page 41.

Pictogram: a visual way of presenting data.

Pie chart: a circular chart divided into parts to show proportions of data.

Primary sources: subjects of study and the raw materials of your work, e.g. a historical document or the text of a poem are both primary sources. See page 82.

Review: a regular recap of work done so far. It's a good idea to start each study session by briefly reviewing the work done last time.

Rubric: the instructions concerning an examination.

Scan: to look for a required detail by running your eye quickly down a page, or over a table of data. See page 62.

Secondary sources: the interpretations, commentaries, essays and books written about the primary sources. See page 82.

Short term memory: the temporary storage of recently learned information in the brain. The information will either be forgotten or transferred to the *long term memory*.

Skim: to gain an idea of what a chapter or book is about. See page 60.

Spray: putting down all your thoughts on a topic and then making links to show relationships between the ideas. See page 40.

SQ3R: a reading strategy for studying a chapter or book. See page 68.

Subject index: an alphabetical list of subjects giving their library code numbers. This index may be on microfiche, in a card catalogue or in a book. See page 50.

Index

Notes

Notes

Notes